D1617007

Telling Their Stories

Telling Their Stories

Puerto Rican Women and Abortion

Jean P. Peterman

WestviewPress

A Division of HarperCollins*Publishers*

Copyright © 1996 by Westview Press, Inc., A Division of HarperCollins Publishers, Inc.

Published in 1996 in the United States of America by Westview Press, Inc., 5500 Central Avenue, Boulder, Colorado 80301-2877, and in the United Kingdom by Westview Press, 12 Hid's Copse Road, Cumnor Hill, Oxford OX2 9JJ

A CIP catalog record for this book is available from the Library of Congress.
ISBN 0-8133-8991-7 (HC)

The paper used in this publication meets the requirements of the American National Standard for Permanence of Paper for Printed Library Materials Z39.48-1984.

10   9   8   7   6   5   4   3   2   1

To the memory of my father

Michael S. Paulson

Contents

Acknowledgments

Many individuals deserve thanks for the completion of this book. I am deeply grateful to all the women who have shared parts of their lives with me. Their personal strengths and insights about their place in the world inspired me to continue my search for other interviewees in spite of dead ends and discouragements.

Kathleen Crittenden, Marisa Alicea, John Johnstone, Anthony Orum, Mary Pellauer, Margaret Strobel and R. Stephen Warner provided helpful critiques at various stages of this research.

The success of this project depended on the usefulness of my interview guide. The guide was improved by suggestions from Roberta Fruth, Leigh Peterman, and especially from Doris Dornberger.

Rosa Bedoya of Network for Youth Services has been generous with her time. Her insights about her work with teen mothers was invaluable. She located both interviewees and persons knowledgeable about the community, and she introduced me to a local restaurant that serves wonderful Puerto Rican food.

This book would not exist in printed form without the help of Bill Peterman, who rescued it at least twice from computer meltdown.

My editor, Jill Rothenberg, provided the support and encouragement I needed to revise and complete the manuscript.

Monetary support for this research was provided by the Rue Bucher Memorial Award administered by the Department of Sociology at the University of Illinois at Chicago and by a grant from the Fahs-Beck Fund for Research and Experimentation.

Jean P. Peterman

1

Introduction

Women in every culture and historical period have used abortion to control their fertility (Smith-Rosenberg 1985). Although the fact of abortion is a constant, the cultural, social and personal experience of abortion is not. This book will focus on the experiences of a particular group of women, Puerto Rican women now living in Chicago, who have at some point in their lives decided to get an abortion.

It may seem surprising that Latina women, including Puerto Rican women, have abortions at a rate one and a half times as high as non-Latinas (Henshaw and Silverman 1988). This high abortion rate coupled with sexually conservative ethnic and religious traditions indicates a cultural contradiction within the Puerto Rican community. A Puerto Rican woman who has an abortion must resolve this contradiction in her own way.

Many Puerto Rican women believe that they must conceal an unplanned pregnancy and an abortion from family members out of respect for these family members. As Jennifer Friedman (1992) demonstrates in her research on teenagers, interdependence and respect for one's parents and other elders characterize Latina families. Respecting one's family for a Latina daughter means not openly disagreeing with her parents' opinions or rules of behavior. As Friedman states, "Latina daughters would rather lie about what they did, than push the boundaries of an elder " (21). She explains that the norm of respect "enables families to survive" (21) and is a source of support. Members of a minority group who are poor are far more likely than poor whites to live in racially or ethnically segregated neighborhoods with a high concentration of poor people (Jargowsky and Bane 1990). The very fact of living in such a neighborhood, and sharing an ethnic and neighborhood culture, may affect how a woman experiences her decision to get an abortion. Additionally, Puerto Rican culture and religious traditions are examples of influences that could make the decision difficult.

A Puerto Rican woman who cannot reveal that she is pregnant may have to resolve her situation without the support of those she needs the most. Additionally, she often lacks cultural support for her decision, and if she is poor, she lacks material resources as well. In spite of these obstacles, the women I interviewed have more than survived. They have made changes in their own lives and the lives of others.

Laurel Richardson's (1990) notion of cultural stories and collective stories provides a useful way of analyzing narratives. According to Richardson, a cultural story provides

> a general understanding of the stock of meanings and their relationship to each other. The process of telling the story creates and supports a social world. Cultural stories provide exemplars of lives, heroes, villains, and fools as they are embedded in larger cultural and social frameworks, as well as stories about home, community, society, and humankind. Morality and cautionary tales instruct the young and control the adult (127).

The cultural story is told from the point of view of the "ruling interests and the normative order" (128). The collective story, in contrast, "displays an individual's story by narrativizing the experiences of the social category to which the individual belongs, rather than by telling the particular individual's story or by simply retelling the cultural story" (128). These collective stories are alternative stories that may emerge through social movement activities or simply by a sharing of experiences.

For example, the mainstream American cultural story is that America is a land of opportunity and anyone who works hard can succeed. The collective story of Puerto Ricans and other communities of color is very different. This story involves struggle against barriers intrinsic to the social structure such as poverty, prejudice and discrimination. The collective story can create a new shared consciousness (Padilla 1985) and the possibility of working for change. For many Puerto Rican women, the cultural story is about virginity, family, motherhood, and male dominance. The collective story in these narratives both modifies and contradicts the cultural story. The collective story is about self-determination and resisting male control. A consistent theme of both the cultural and collective stories is the interdependence and respect that characterize Puerto Rican family life.

Reflexivity and Research

In creating, doing, and writing about this research, I am situating myself in the reflexive tradition (e.g. Stacey 1990, 1991; Gluck, Berger, and Patai, 1991; Warner 1988; Stanley and Wise 1991, 1993.) Stanley and

Wise (1993) explain that reflexive research "must be concerned with the experience and consciousness of the researcher as an essential part of the research process" (28). They go on to explain that

> ... all research involves, at its basis, an interaction, a relationship, between researcher and researched. We also believe that such a relationship exists whether 'the researched' are books, secondary data, other objects, or people. Because the basis of all research is a relationship, this necessarily involves the presence of the researcher *as a person* (161, emphasis in original).

My presence "as a person" in this research includes my political work in the feminist and abortion rights movements, my belief that these movements should be racially and ethnically inclusive, and the fact that I am a middle class white female.

Most of my involvement with feminist advocacy since the mid-1970's has centered around some aspect of abortion rights: maintaining its legality, maintaining access to it, and creating a climate of public acceptance of the idea that legal abortion is essential to women's well-being. Over the years, friends and acquaintances have sometimes shared their stories of unplanned pregnancies with me. These stories were prefaced with statements to the effect that they have kept what they were about to tell me a secret, that there are very few people they trust enough to talk about this with, and because of my political commitment and my personal (empathetic) style, they want to share their stories with me. Of course, in order to respect my friends' privacy, I had to forget these stories as soon as I heard them. This experience made me want to know more about how women were actually experiencing what I was working for politically.

For my initial study (Peterman 1990) I interviewed working- and middle-class white women who were patients at a Chicago-area abortion clinic. From the semi-structured personal interviews I conducted with fifteen women, it was clear that each respondent thought of her abortion decision as one that was embedded in her own life, rather than as an abstract moral issue. Her decision most often involved a choice between two distinct futures. Several themes emerged that characterize the meaning of abortion for these women: reclaiming a satisfying life, preventing a crushing burden on an already unstable life, exercising power in the relationship, and nurturing the relationship. Women's beliefs about relationships, children, and careers shaped, and were shaped by, the abortion experience. Additionally, the seven women who were practicing Catholics had to come to terms with the fact that getting an abortion was in direct opposition to the teaching of their church. For my Catholic interviewees, being Catholic did not necessarily contribute to the difficulty of the decision. Three said they experienced it as easy and four experienced it as difficult.

Women for whom the abortion decision came most easily experienced it as an act of assertion, either to reclaim a life that they liked or to exercise power in the relationship. The experience of these women is at odds with public attitudes about abortion. The public is most accepting of abortion when the woman is a victim of difficult circumstances (General Social Survey 1988). My results are consistent with poll data in suggesting that women who are happy with their lives and are not willing to change them are what the abortion controversy is really about (see also Luker 1984, Gordon 1986). For women for whom the abortion was an act of assertion, the decision was a way of saying that their lives and their needs are important.

This research takes place during a time when abortion is a hotly contested political and social issue. The U.S. Supreme Court's rulings in *Webster v. Reproductive Health Services* (1989) and *Casey v. Planned Parenthood of Southeast Pennsylvania* (1992) mean that individual states are free to enact barriers to abortion such as consent laws and waiting periods. Additionally, anti-abortion activists are staging blockades at abortion clinics throughout the nation in an attempt to intimidate patients and staff and to create publicity for their point of view. Nevertheless, public support for legal abortion remains high. A Harris Poll taken immediately after the Webster decision indicated that "a record high 61-37 percent of the public now supports the original Roe v. Wade decision" (Harris 1990).

The political and social context in which abortion occurs includes the fact that abortion was legalized throughout the United States in 1973, during a period of feminist activism. Legal abortion thus occurs in a context of expanded opportunities for women. Safe, available methods of contraception and legal, accessible abortion make it possible for women to postpone or reject marriage and childbearing in favor of school or work, and to integrate childbearing into a life that includes other possibilities. In general, a woman need no longer derive her status from the man she marries. Personal and social ambivalence about female self-determination fuels the public controversy over abortion.

Research on Abortion

The literature on abortion, in general, consists of historical accounts (Mohr 1978; Degler 1985; Gordon 1977; Solinger 1994), moral arguments for or against the procedure (Callahan and Callahan 1984; Harrison 1983; Noonan 1970; Maguire 1983; Pyne Parsons 1978), and research on attitudes about abortion (Luker 1984; Scott and Schuman 1988; Plutzer 1988; Granberg and Granberg 1980). With few exceptions (notably Solinger 1994, Harrison 1983 and Pyne Parsons 1978), in literature of this type abortion is generally treated as an ethical issue abstracted from women's lives.

Relatively little work has been done on women's experience with an unplanned pregnancy and the decision to get an abortion. Researchers have conducted interviews with abortion patients in order to analyze their moral development (Gilligan 1982), discover reasons why they did not use contraceptives (Luker 1975), and uncover stories about the danger and humiliation of illegal abortion (Messer and May 1988; Miller 1993). While only Gilligan examined the decision-making process itself, in all of these accounts it is clear that the decision to abort was not made ahead of time, in the abstract, but in response to a concrete set of circumstances. Women often experience deciding to get an abortion as a choice between two very different futures.

One recent study of abortion patients (Torres and Forrest 1988) deals more directly with the decision-making process. At least half of all respondents in this study said they had relationship problems or did not want to be single parents; two-thirds said they were unable to afford a child; and three-quarters were concerned about how having a baby would change their lives. All of these reasons illustrate the real life dilemmas that women must resolve.

Rosalind Petchesky (1985) argues that "a theory and analysis of the social relations of reproduction is necessary to make concrete the idea of reproduction as a domain that constructs women as a gender and women's own consciousness" (ix). She shows that reproductive behavior has two dimensions, a personal one and a social one. At the personal level, decisions about sexuality, contraception and abortion are individual ones, and depend on specific personal circumstances. These matters have a social dimension as well. Reproductive behavior is conditioned by social reality: class, race, and the existing division of labor between the sexes. Reproductive behavior is not innate, it is socially constructed, and as any given social situation changes, the reproductive behavior of individuals may change as well.

Some women take their right to a safe, legal abortion for granted, while others may be affected by the intense social controversy generated by this issue. Abortion as a subject for public debate is a recent phenomenon. During the approximately one hundred years that abortions were illegal in the United States, women continued to get them, but the need for abortion was considered a private, secret problem.

In a study conducted at an abortion clinic, Louise Howe (1984) interviewed clinic personnel, patients, and their companions, and observed group counseling sessions. She also interviewed political activists and describes the work of an organizer for Catholics for a Free Choice who went door to door in an older, predominantly Italian and Irish section of Brooklyn:

> Initially she had expected doors to be slammed in her face, since the women who lived behind them were precisely the kind of older, traditional, church going Catholics most likely to say in public that abortion is always a mortal sin. But in the privacy of their kitchens and living rooms, after their young neighbor presented her case, an amazing proportion began to pour out remembrances, sometimes of their own abortions, sometimes of their sisters' or cousins' or older childhood friends'. Over the years, they told the young organizer, they had entrusted the truth to only a very few. And also over the years, the organizer learned, among similar kinds of Catholic women in many parts of the world, a special secret term was often used in private instead of the unmentionable word abortion. The term was 'making angels' (117).

Abortion continues to be a secret problem for many Latinas (Espin 1984).

Regardless of the secrecy of abortion in individual women's lives, abortion today is a very public phenomenon and the meaning of abortion is highly contested. Opponents of abortion name it murder. A central strategy of anti-abortion activists is to confront the general public, and especially abortion patients, with an image of the fetus, so that the reality of fetal personhood becomes a "self-fulfilling prophecy by making the fetus a *public presence*" (Petchesky 1987, emphasis in original). Political activity directed at abortion clinic patients and personnel is an ongoing reality. While such activity adds to the stress of obtaining an abortion, it has not affected the number of abortions erformed (Forrest and Henshaw 1987).

Other groups give different meanings to abortion. Civil libertarians refer to it as a privacy right. Feminists claim that a woman has a right to control her body and to determine her own life plan. Many opinion polls implicitly assume that abortion is a necessary evil, with questions that suggest that an abortion needs to be justified by one of a list of circumstances, such as rape or poverty. While the women in both my earlier (1990) study and this study used some of this language, it does not capture the essence of what was really going on. The definition of abortion that comes closest to how these women talked about it is Barbara Katz Rothman's (1989) woman-centered one:

> An abortion at, say, ten weeks may mean different things to different women, and different things to the same woman in different pregnancies. One woman schedules an abortion with less emotional involvement than she has in scheduling dental work. Another schedules an

abortion and begins a lifelong grieving for the death of her baby. Is this the contradiction it appears to be? No, not if we take a genuinely women-centered view of pregnancy and abortion and recognize that abortion, like pregnancy itself, takes its meaning from the woman in whose body the pregnancy is unfolding (106-107).

In view of how controversial abortion is as a social issue, it is important to begin to understand women's experience of it. It is equally important to understand that women's experiences may be influenced by their race, ethnicity, and class. The major focus of this research, on Puerto Rican women, is an attempt to highlight both the diversity and similarity of these experiences.

Moving Puerto Rican Women to the Center

Feminism as a political movement and feminist scholarship have been strengthened by critiques of previously excluded women, especially women of color and lesbians (e.g. hooks 1984; Moraga and Anzaldua 1981). These women have suggested (or demanded) that their concerns be moved "from the margin to the center" (hooks 1984) of feminist theory and activism. They challenged the idea that the experience of white, middle class, heterosexual women represents the experience of all women. Writing about research on the family, Maxine Baca Zinn (1989, 1990) argues that neither the feminist or the racial critique of the family is sufficient, and that inclusive research about relationships and family life must pay attention to race, class, and gender.

This research places a traditionally excluded group, Puerto Rican women, at its center. As someone who is not Puerto Rican I have felt, throughout the research process, some misgivings about using my academic authority to "represent" these women. African-American feminist bell hooks (1989) provides a helpful perspective on white women writing about women of color. She has several concerns. One is that, owing to race privilege, white women's work about women of color will be viewed by others as more authoritative than work by women of color. Another concern is that some white women have simply abdicated their responsibility for inclusive scholarship, believing, for example, that only Puerto Ricans should write about other Puerto Ricans. Hooks believes that it is important that scholars write about people other than themselves, while being aware that their point of view is partial. She states that "[c]ross-ethnic feminist scholarship should emphasize the value of a scholar's work as well as the unique perspective that scholar brings to bear on the subject" (48). She explains that "[s]uch a position would allow white women scholars to share their ideas about black women's writing (or any group of women's writing) without assuming that their thoughts would be seen as 'definitive' or that they were trying to be 'the authority' " (48). This research, then, is about Puerto Rican women from the point of view of a white middle class woman, and is not meant as the only possible representation of them.

Puerto Rican Women

Puerto Rico is unique in that it is neither fully incorporated into the U.S. as a state, nor is it an independent nation: it functions as a colony of the United States. One result of this fact is that Puerto Rico has often served as a laboratory for American policies or products. For example, beginning in the 1950's, U.S. manufacturing firms experimented in Puerto Rico with production policies that generated a strong demand for low wage, often female, workers (Rios 1990). The expansion of these policies world-wide by U.S. capitalists has led to the development of a "global assembly-line" of very low paid women workers who often must work long hours under dangerous conditions (Enloe 1989; Rios 1990).

Almost from the beginning of the U.S. colonization of Puerto Rico, population was considered a problem by the U.S. (Ramirez de Arellano and Seipp 1983). Annette Ramirez de Arellano and Conrad Seipp explain that two solutions to the population "problem" were pursued: promotion of migration to the U.S. and population control policies in Puerto Rico. They state that U.S. pharmaceutical companies used Puerto Rican women to test the birth control pill, Emko foam, I.U.D.'s, and Depro-Provera. Further, in 1976, 35% of all Puerto Rican women of childbearing age had been sterilized. On the other hand, most women in Puerto Rico did not have access to contraception. Many women became sterilized after bearing more children than they had wanted. Currently, abortion is legal and available in Puerto Rico and sterilization rates have gone down, yet sterilization remains the primary option for many poor women who do not have access to other means of controlling fertility (Ramirez de Arrellano and Seipp 1983).

The first Puerto Ricans who came to the U.S. mainland settled in New York. After World War II, Puerto Ricans began to move to Chicago, and now there are neighborhoods with large concentration of Puerto Ricans, namely, Humboldt Park, West Town, and Logan Square (Padilla 1985). According to the U.S. Census, Puerto Ricans are near the bottom in per capita income, years of college completed for men, and male earnings, and near the top in per cent of population in households with incomes below the poverty level (Farley 1991). Puerto Ricans have the highest poverty rates among minorities in general and among Latino minorities as well, and this is true for Puerto Ricans in Chicago as well as Puerto Ricans nationwide (Robles 1988). Jennifer Robles points out that "the Puerto Rican poverty rate in Cook County was 31.6 percent, compared to 17.5 percent for Mexicans and 10.5 percent for Cubans," and that "the 16.7 percent infant mortality rate for Puerto Ricans in Chicago for the combined years of 1982-1983 was far above the Mexican rate of 9.5 percent" (Robles 1988:9). Census figures indicate that about 27% of Puerto Rican households reported receiving public assistance, compared to 14.4% of all Hispanic households (Casuso and Camacho 1985). Of particular importance for the issue of reproductive behavior in general is the fact that Puerto Ricans, like other Hispanics, are youthful, with a median age for Puerto Ricans of twenty-one (Casuso and Camacho 1985). A high proportion of the population is thus in the stage of life when parenthood is most likely.

In general, the model for assimilation of ethnic groups in the U.S. suggests that over several generations, as members of various groups learn English well enough to speak it comfortably, use of the language of origin drops off and eventually disappears (Bakalian 1993). However, Puerto Ricans in the U.S. do not fit this model. They generally remain both bi-lingual and bi-cultural (Rodriguez 1991).

A recurrent problem for women of any disadvantaged ethnic group is the conflict between her needs as a woman and cultural norms (the cultural story) of male dominance. A Puerto Rican woman may be told that it is in the best interests of the Puerto Rican community as a whole to remain silent about issues of gender. Some women accept this while others do not. Puerto Rican writer Lydia Vegas (1984) asks, "what if one of those so called National Values [we're supposed to defend] just happens to be sexism?" (45). Writing about colonized women in the third world, Cynthia Enloe (1989) explains the power of cultural norms, such as the veiling of Muslim women, as symbols to resistance to Westernization this way:

> Men in many communities appear to assign such ideological weight to the outward attire and sexual purity of women in the community because they see women as (1) the community's — or the nation's — most valuable *possessions*; (2) the principle vehicles for transmitting the whole nation's values from one generation to the next; (3) bearers of the communities future generations — crudely, nationalist wombs; (4) the members of the community most vulnerable to defilement and exploitation by oppressive alien rulers; and (5) most susceptible to assimilation and cooptation by insidious outsiders (54, emphasis in original).

Armenian feminist Arlene Avakian (1988) suggests that male insistence on patriarchal norms as definitional for a particular culture may ultimately be self-defeating. Her discussions with Armenian young people revealed that

> what was articulated both by some of the young women in the discussion and one young man is that the Armenian community is also threatened by not changing its patriarchal traditions. Simply put, the young women who want so much to carry on Armenian culture might not be willing to sacrifice themselves in order to contribute to the continuity of the race (2-3).

The use of contraception and abortion is often a focus of the conflict between a woman's well being and cultural expectations about her behavior. In this context, the distinction between reproductive health care as essential to women's well-being and self-determination, as opposed to population control as a form of imperialism, is a critical one (Hartmann 1987). Third world nations and communities of color are on the receiving end of population control programs (Hartmann 1987). Recall that Puerto Rican women in Puerto Rico and on the mainland have been subject to an intensive sterilization campaign and that U.S. pharmaceutical companies have used Puerto Rican women to test several kinds of contraception (Ramirez de Arellano and Seipp 1983). Conservative members of communities of color often collapse the distinction between population control and reproductive rights, claiming that the availability of contraception and abortion is "genocide." White dominated pro-choice groups, on the other hand, often do not recognize the importance of the distinction and fail to dissociate themselves from population control ideology (some exceptions are Latinas for Reproductive Choice; the Women of Color Partnership Program, Religious Coalition for Abortion Rights; the Latina Initiative, Catholics for a Free Choice; the Inclusivity Project of the Illinois Pro-Choice Alliance; and CARASA [Committee for Abortion Rights and Against Sterilization Abuse]). While population control policies attempt to limit the fertility of certain women, patriarchal and pronatalist policies attempt to deny women access to contraception and abortion. The common thread in both policies is that women's needs are ignored, and women are denied control of their reproductive capacity.

The narratives of the twenty women I interviewed for this study indicate the strength of the cultural story in their lives. Yet for some respondents, their abortion experience served as a "moral passage" (Addelson 1991) to the beginning of a collective (oppositional) story. A collective story, however, cannot create the possibility for change unless it is shared. Some women are beginning to create spaces in their families, with their daughters, or in their personal or public lives, for the collective story to be told. These women reject the idea of male control and value personal goals for themselves. Nevertheless, they maintain a strong Puerto Rican identity, including a family life characterized by interdependence and respect, and a commitment to the Puerto Rican community.

2

The Meaning of Abortion

Each of the twenty women in some way integrated the decision to get an abortion into her entire life, including her personal goals and her relationships. She considered, briefly or at length, what her life would be like if she did or did not get the abortion. Building on Barbara Katz Rothman's (1989) idea that an abortion takes its meaning from the woman who is pregnant, I analyzed the narratives for patterns of meaning. Throughout the interview process, four categories emerged that characterize the meaning of abortion for individual women: "keeping on being who I was," preserving life or health, coping with physical or emotional abandonment, and resisting or escaping male control. For some women, the abortion had more than one meaning.

"Keeping on Being Who I Was"

Having an abortion was "the only solution to keeping on being who I was -- a teenager who wants to finish high school," explained Rosa (all names are pseudonyms). She added that at the time she discovered her pregnancy, she "was just starting to live." When Rosa told her boyfriend she was pregnant, he was happy and offered support. Rosa, however, had reason to believe that this boy "wanted a housewife," while Rosa wanted to finish high school and go on to study nursing. She was not able to share the fact of her pregnancy with her strict Catholic parents, but she confided in her older sister, who had gotten pregnant at the age of eighteen and had to leave home and marry the father. The older sister apparently regretted this and insisted to Rosa that abortion was her best alternative. The lack of any real discussion made Rosa's abortion difficult. She "would go to bed crying" and she was "angry at my sister for not giving me enough time to think." Rosa described conflicting feelings of "selfishness" because she "would be doing something bad" over against the realization that she "never did want a kid," and that abortion was "the only solution to keeping on being who I was -- a teenager who wants to finish high school."

For each of twelve women, terminating her pregnancy meant that she could keep on being who she was. For eight of these women, a major part of "who she was" involved continuing her education.

Evelyn was in her second year of college when she discovered her pregnancy. Her boyfriend expected her to continue the pregnancy and marry him, but she had other ideas:

> I was in college. That was a big deal for me. The most important thing in my life was to graduate, to be a role-model to my brothers and my sisters. And I didn't love this person. ... There wasn't even a question in my mind.

Evelyn's boyfriend felt hurt by the abortion. He was a high school drop-out and didn't understand her desire to study. When Evelyn got a second abortion shortly after her graduation, he broke off the relationship.

Alicia was also a college student, and married, when she discovered her pregnancy. She and her husband were "just getting along," working, attending class, and participating in social and political activities with other Puerto Rican students. Alicia's husband suggested the abortion. Although she believes that it was the right decision, she regrets that she didn't have more time to think about it:

> The first thing I wanted to do was keep the baby, but my husband was very opposed to that because of our financial situation. We could barely make it ourselves. After thinking about it some more, I was convinced of that also, but it was a very difficult decision to make.

She went on to explain that the idea of having a baby was "the most frightening thing. If I had decided not to have the abortion, either him or I would have had to quit school and gotten a real job to support the three of us." Alicia still thinks of her abortion as "a little hurt," and explained how it has changed her thinking: "I know what making the decision is like. I can empathize with another woman in the same situation."

Alicia said that she has participated in defending an abortion clinic in Chicago against harassment by anti-abortion activists, and that she would be willing to speak at a pro-choice rally. Despite her political stance, she has never told her mother, who lives in Puerto Rico, about the abortion, nor has she told many of her friends:

> As much as I like to think I am over my upbringing, if I'm honest with you, I still would not mention the fact that I've had an abortion with

some of my closest friends. ... because I guess it is sort of a shameful thing, even though I do feel comfortable with it.

Evelyn shares some of Alicia's conflict between her adult beliefs and her upbringing. At the time she got her abortion, Evelyn "had some Marxist beliefs -- I was for revolution," and she believed that abortion should be "a woman's choice." Nevertheless,

> It was so painful for me to do that, even though I knew that's what I wanted. Just the fact that I went ahead to do something that is so against my family and our values, our traditions, and our norms, I said, 'Well Evelyn, you're on your own now, and you have to be strong.'

The conflict that Evelyn experienced between her upbringing in a traditional Puerto Rican culture and her needs as a Puerto Rican woman is a common theme in these narratives.

Most women with a concern about education were concerned about their own. Marisol, however, was concerned about her daughter's. When asked to describe her life shortly before she discovered she was pregnant, she replied simply, "it was fine." Marisol is a single mother of two girls, ages fifteen and ten. She never finished high school, and she supports herself and the girls with her job as the manager of a leather goods store and with child support from her former husband. She explained what having a baby would have meant to her family:

> I started planning what nurseries I would need. I couldn't leave my job. My oldest daughter would have to pick up the baby because nurseries close at 6:00 or 6:30, and care for the baby. [Then I thought] what am I doing? This is not her child, its my baby. She couldn't join her sports anymore. For me to love my baby, and have my baby would just stop their lives. Here I am trying to make a livelihood, trying to show her, please finish high school, please finish college. I would do it all over again. I would make sure I had my education. What am I showing her? I am showing her 'you can take care of a child and go to school' but I don't want that for her. That was my first realization. She would be more parent than I would be. She would lose her teenage life because of something that was my doing.

Marisol said that she didn't think her abortion was the right decision, then added that it was "the best decision."

"I enjoyed my freedom of being alone, of making choices for myself," is the way Lupe described her life as a rebellious fifteen year old living in Puerto Rico. Lupe had dropped out of school and left her parents' home to live with "a large group of rebels, a very experimental group, into heavy metal without losing touch of our culture -- Spanish speaking heavy metal Salsa rock and roll." When Lupe realized she was pregnant, she "didn't know who the father was," did not tell anyone, and somehow got together enough money to come to her grandmother's home in Chicago. Lupe "didn't tell her I was coming, I just showed up one night at 2:00 a.m." When asked why she came all the way to Chicago for an abortion, Lupe replied that "it's such a secret, I thought it wasn't legal in Puerto Rico." Without telling anyone, she looked up the address of Planned Parenthood in the phone book and scheduled her abortion the next week. She eventually graduated from an alternative high school in Chicago, where she now teaches.

These women who had abortions to keep on being who they were -- students, employed single mothers, women whose families were complete -- form the largest group. Although six of the twelve experienced their decision as difficult, each of them believes it was the best decision.

Preserving Life or Health

To preserve life or health is one of the most socially acceptable reasons for obtaining an abortion. A majority of American adults believe that a woman should be able to obtain an abortion for health reasons (General Social Survey 1988). Yet this generalized acceptability was not enough to overcome Helena's Catholic upbringing, even though she no longer attends mass.

Right after the birth of her last child, Helena was advised, for medical reasons, not to have another baby. When she went to confirm this pregnancy, to "a doctor that I trusted, he stressed that the choice was losing me or losing the baby or losing both." Helena was not able to share this decision with anyone but her husband. She especially did not want to tell her mother, who is "very religious -- she's a Charismatic Catholic." Helena believes she made the right decision about her pregnancy. She has informally counseled other women about unplanned pregnancies, and she has even appeared on television, with her identity concealed, to advocate a pro-choice position. With all of this, her own ambivalence remains: "Every time you kiss the baby, you think, because I want to care for [this baby] you have to sacrifice another life."

Coping With Emotional or Physical Abandonment

In some relationships, an unplanned pregnancy creates a crisis that precipitates the end of the relationship or drastically changes the nature of the relationship. A woman in this situation must then consider whether or not she can raise a child without male support. For seven of the twenty women, their abortion was in some way related to emotional or physical abandonment by their male partner. For two of these, Marisol and Lucy, their abortions were both a means of coping with abandonment and keeping on being who they were.

When Marisol told her partner she was pregnant, he let her know that he was unwilling to move in with her, marry her, or be a father to the child. It was at this point that Marisol realized that, for her daughters, having a baby "would have stopped their lives," and her own. Lucy and her partner had already left each other when she discovered her pregnancy, and Lucy saw her decision as "deciding either on having another child and living off public aid or going back to school and getting a decent job and raising my first son." Four of the remaining women who were coping with male abandonment did not state that the abortion was also related to personal goals.

Gloria was a communications major working at a local radio station, and her partner, with whom she lived, was in medical school. Gloria stated that her partner "didn't seem ruffled by the pregnancy" and told her "we'll just get married," but Gloria sensed that something was wrong:

> He didn't act like he knew about how it would change, and how he would help, and would I have to keep it quiet because of his lack of support. I was asking for *us* to have a plan. Now, maybe I just didn't think he would be a good father, that I would be getting any help.

Gloria thinks she was especially sensitive to her partner's emotional distance from raising a child because of her own experience as an "accident:"

> I can't give it everything. It needs a father. I was thinking about my own father. About six months before I was born, my parents had their first grandson. I was always fighting for my father's attention.

"Not being just a doctor's wife" was of concern to Gloria, and she did have personal goals. However, she explained that at the time of her pregnancy, she was close to finishing her own degree and her parents would have supported her. Although having a baby would have "slowed me down," it wouldn't have derailed her.

Unfortunately, Gloria's sense of her partner's emotional immaturity was borne out by subsequent events. Shortly after the abortion, Gloria and her partner got married, and he graduated from medical school. A year later, her husband had lined up a residency in a New York hospital and she had lined up a job there also. The relationship was not going well. The night before they both were to leave for New York, they had an argument, and Gloria's husband informed her that she was not coming with him, unpacked all her belongings, threw the apartment keys at her, and drove off. She has not seen him again, and he filed for divorce in New York. Gloria stated that "only recently, in the last year, have I come to the acceptance that me and my husband aren't going to work it out." She describes her life now as "definitely better, I've come out of a living hell."

Cherrie's narrative provides a complex account of the interaction of her mother's death from an illegal abortion, her own problematic relationships, and her Baptist faith in creating regret for her two abortions coupled with her belief that abortion should be legal and available.

Cherrie was born and raised in Puerto Rico. Shortly after her birth, her mother got pregnant again, and, "somebody came to the house. At that time they used a lady [as an abortionist]. So my mother died at the age of twenty-six. She lost all her blood."

Cherrie did not learn the cause of her mother's death until she was a teenager. Meanwhile, her father had also died and she was being raised by her grandparents, who were so strict that Cherrie ran away from home and came to Chicago to live with an uncle. Soon afterward, she married a man who abused her:

> I was an orphan, always looking for protection. Nobody looked like they liked me. I was afraid to open the refrigerator in my uncle's house. So I found this guy, and had my own little apartment. I wasn't even thinking about guys. Mentally I was like a little girl, coming from a small village in Puerto Rico. He took advantage of that. 'Here's the Puerto Rican hillbilly.' This guy was hitting me. It was terrible, but I was pregnant. After that, I was by myself.

Cherrie left this relationship and got a job to support herself and her baby daughter. She says that she and her daughter "grew up together."

Cherrie became pregnant again when her daughter was fourteen. The man with whom she got pregnant made the decision to end the pregnancy, located the clinic, and took Cherrie there. She did not question any of this because, "it would be hard for me, if this guy didn't want this baby. I already had one baby by myself, and another one?"

Years later, Cherrie had another abortion, which was "completely the opposite of the other time. This time, it was me that wanted the abortion and he wanted the baby." He was a new partner, not yet divorced from his first wife, and Cherrie could not be sure that the relationship would be permanent.

Eventually they did get married, and shortly afterwards, Cherrie got pregnant again, but miscarried. She stated that she regrets both her abortions, that there is "an emptiness in the house," and described her longing for commitment:

You get angry with God, that I try to do things right, find the right person to love me and make a commitment with God, and have a house, and for the person to be honest, and then to find out later it was 'just for a while.' In the case of my husband, it was not exactly that, it was just that it was the wrong moment for that, because he was not divorced yet, and going through a lot of things. At that time it was even worse, because he wanted me to have that baby so bad. He was screaming at me, and crying. He got like that because he wanted that baby so bad. And then it was me -- no, no, no. I went all by myself. Right after, the day after, I went back to work, with nobody knowing.

Cherrie was raised Baptist in Puerto Rico and now attends a Baptist church in Chicago that is well known for political activity against abortion. Although she regrets both of her abortions, she believes that abortion should be legal and she thinks her mother would not have died if she had had a medical abortion. She explained that

Everybody has to do whatever they think. It's not good to have an abortion, but the way that we live, with teenagers and so many problems, they're going to find somebody to do it.

Although Cherrie regrets her abortions, she knows that for some women, "it doesn't hurt emotionally." When asked if she would condemn these women, she said "no."

Cherrie clearly separated her own feelings from the experience of other women who do not regret their abortions. She also separated her own relationship with God from her relationship with her church, in that her relationship "is with God, not with the church," and "it's their opinion -- this is me." She added that

I was feeling guilty. Things are going to be worse because I did that. ... Then I went through a depression, a very bad depression, and little by little, I understand that He forgives me, that I have to live. I can't deal with that by myself. I leave that to God.

Although thirteen of the twenty women described their abortion decision as difficult, all but two believe it was the best decision. Both of these women, Cherrie and Ana (Ana's story follows), terminated their pregnancies as a way of coping with male abandonment. Each of their narratives indicate that the emotional hurt of a broken relationship contributed to their regret, and that each abortion represented the failure of the relationship.

Ana described a very difficult period of her life as the context for her abortion:

I had three kids already, and I thought I had too many kids, that it was a lot of work. It's [the abortion] from the father of my three kids also. We had a lot of problems. He had a drinking problem. Almost always, I was alone with the kids [ages 3, 4 and 7]. We had a lot of fights. He would work and drink everything. I thought there was going to be more problems. I didn't have his help, so I decided that was the best thing, [so I] don't have to be hiding with the kids when he came home drunk, in my neighbors house.

In spite of what seems an overwhelming situation, Ana claims that if she hadn't told her partner right away that she was pregnant, she would have had the baby. She resents his part in the abortion:

That's why I did it, because he had a reaction like he didn't want to help me, and so then I got mad, because he didn't help me for anything else, but he looked for the money [for the abortion]. He didn't help me for the other kids, but he looked for the money. I thought 'I hope he doesn't get the money.' I didn't really want to do it. But he got the money, so I thought I had to do it. He didn't tell me not to.

Manuel took Ana for her abortion, and when he returned to pick her up

I was crying and crying. When he came to pick me up I wouldn't talk to him. When he took me to my house, I told him to leave, that I didn't want to see him. ... so I didn't see him for six months after. I didn't want to do it. I think it's his fault.

Ana went on to say that her fourth child, now two years old, is by the same man. This time, when she told him she was pregnant

He was happy. He knew I still cried for my baby. I asked him, 'do you want it?' He said 'Don't you dare do nothing to that baby.' He was sorry for the baby we lost. He gave me this one.

Manuel backed up his words of support with action. He stopped drinking. He stays with the two-year old while Ana works at her sub-minimum wage, cash only job in the "underground economy." At the time of the interview, Ana lived with her four children in temporary housing provided by a social service agency. She was having trouble finding a job with adequate pay and an affordable apartment. When asked about her relationship with Manuel, Ana replied,"I still love him. I don't want nobody in my life. He's been my only husband. I don't want to be with another person." Likewise, Manuel doesn't want to lose me or the four kids, but we always remember the abortion. We always remember it. [What do you mean?] When we try to be together, or talk, or start a life again, I always tell him that [about the abortion] and then we start fighting. ... When he wants to come back to me, I tell him that, inside, he's no good because he made me do it. If he had loved me like he says, he would have told me he would support me. He said it was the drinking problem that made him do that.

Ana blames her abortion on her partner, abortion clinic personnel, and even the fact that abortion is legal: "[They] shouldn't have those places, so easy for you to go to. They don't tell you stop and think about it, they're just interested in the money, they ruin your life, they don't help you, I hate them." She has never been able to talk about her abortion with anyone in her family and she says that she has hardly any friends.

Ana was one of five women located through a "personal" ad. When she called to find out more about the interview, she told me she lived in temporary housing and not reachable by phone, and set up a meeting for 8:00 that evening at a small restaurant located in a neighborhood widely perceived as dangerous. I waited in the tiny entrance way until 8:45. I did not enter the restaurant because all of the patrons were Puerto Rican men, and I thought my presence would affect their conversations. Occasionally, one of the men would use the telephone next to where I was standing. One man assured me that he was "a good husband," calling to let his wife know where he was.

Two days later, Ana telephoned me again, apologized for having to work late, and said she really wanted to do the interview. She insisted that the same tiny restaurant would be an appropriate place, so I again agreed to meet her there. She arrived with a man, who left when I assured them that I would drive Ana home afterwards. During the interview, Ana told me that "the man who brought me here -- it's him [the father of the four children]." She said he speaks only Spanish, which explained his puzzled look as I was offering to drive Ana home. I followed Ana's suggestions about what to order for our dinner, and we completed the interview.

At the end of our conversation Ana told me that the reason she was so eager to do the interview with me is that she has never had anyone to talk to about her abortion:

When I saw this in the newspaper, I got really happy. [Why is that?] because I never had talked to nobody, so I said, 'here is my chance to talk.' I got real happy and when I couldn't meet you I said 'oh, she's not going to trust me no more, she's not going to call me no more,' because I didn't come here. I thought you were going to forget about it. But then in the store, they gave me another newspaper and then I saw it again, and I was real happy and then I called you again.

Before we left the restaurant, Ana showed me pictures of her four children.

Resisting or Escaping Male Control

For four women resisting or escaping male control was a central feature of the abortion experience. For one woman, Rosa, her abortion allowed her to "keep on being who I was," in part because she sensed, even as a teenager, that her boyfriend wanted a housewife. In fact, she married him a year later and divorced him shortly afterward because "he was from the old school." When asked to explain, she said,

> you know what 'barefoot and pregnant' is? [yes] He didn't want me to work or go to school. He tried to lock me out [of life]. I went to DeVry for six months without telling him. I would hurry home to cook dinner. When he found out [I was going to DeVry], it started our divorce.

Rosa was also taking birth control pills during that time, without her husband's knowledge, and he found out about the pills about the same time he found out about DeVry. In summing up this relationship, Rosa said, "he just wanted me to cook. He didn't care about my opinion."

Sylvia married when she was sixteen. Shortly after their son was born, Sylvia wanted to go to night school. She told me that her husband promised to watch the baby, so she signed the contract. When the time came for her to leave for school, he asked who would watch the baby, and refused to do so himself. For Sylvia, "that just blew my plans off." When asked about her friends, Sylvia replied

> my husband never wanted me to associate with any of my friends. I had a limited time to talk to them, and visiting was out of the question, unless he was present. So my relationship with my friends grew apart. I had no social life and still don't. I needed my friends. Now, everything I have to say, I say to my husband, but he's not a good listener. He has a bad temper -- not physically, but he just has a short temper.

Sylvia's husband attempted to extend his control over her when she told him she was pregnant again. He accused her of being unfaithful:

> He denied everything [that he was the father of the child]. That really hurt me, it was an easy way to cop out. I thought he was ready for another kid. That's why I was confused. I couldn't think of why he denied it.

Sylvia "didn't want to bring another child into this world whose daddy wasn't going to love him." The meaning of her abortion for Sylvia encompasses both this category and the previous one. That is, she was coping with emotional abandonment by her husband and this emotional abandonment was an attempt to increase his control over her behavior.

In the course of deciding what to do about her pregnancy, Sylvia did take up with another man, someone she met while she was alone, trying to figure out what to do.

> I went out one night and found this man friend, so he knew, and he was the only supportive person that I could even trust. He even went down [to the abortion clinic] with me. I met him by accident. I went out to get a cup of coffee and be by myself, and he was there. He approached me and asked me what was wrong and I told him something different and he sat down at my table and we talked. He asked if he could see me again and I said 'sure.' A week passed and I was growing anxious about what to do. My husband said if I was going to keep it, he wasn't going to be too supportive. I was confused and this man helped me through my confusion.

Eventually, said Sylvia, "I did get into a relationship with him." After the abortion

> I left [my husband] several times. The first time was with this guy. He was so supportive, totally different. It was so strange. I thought, 'I don't know any guys who are like this, or any men,' 'cause he was a man. He offered me so many things, bought me a car, clothes, my son clothes. I thought that 'I don't deserve this.' I think the relationship broke off when my husband found out about it. He started threatening me. He called and threatened to kill me and Jaime.

Sylvia has moved out and been with other men several times. Each time, her husband has threatened to kill her and their son. Sylvia said that

> things were never the same. Every year things got worse and worse, and they're still getting worse. There's no trust. This relationship I have now is just for Jaime's sake. He loves his Dad. He wants us to be together.

At one point, the husband was staying with his mother. Sylvia called her mother-in-law and told her about the threats. Sylvia stated that the threats have stopped, but later in the interview she suggested otherwise:

> whatever he does, it doesn't have an impact on me anymore like it used to. Before, when he told me he couldn't watch Jaime, I thought, 'one

day Jaime is going to grow up, and that's going to be my time.' Meanwhile I've got to hang on and accept him. The things I would never accept from a man are physical abuse. That I have never gotten from him. He used to threaten me. Now, I threaten him. When he threatens me and talks all the violence, I call the cops, and there they are.

Sylvia was the only respondent to describe her current relationship as abusive. I gave her the name of a social service agency geared toward Latinas in case she decided to seek outside help.

Although I had encountered illegal abortion through reading and films, I was not prepared for the emotional intensity of a face to face conversation with a woman telling me how she almost died. Two women had abortions prior to 1973. Each of them was escaping male violence or control.

Caroline got married at seventeen to a man she says would not let her finish high school, confined her to the house, and prevented her from having any contact with her friends or her family. She was soon pregnant.

> And the man that I was supposed to love, I started to hate him. Not only because he jeopardized my dreams, but he made it worse for me by making me pregnant.

When she had the baby, "my dreams were there, but now I knew I would have to wait." When she got pregnant again, in 1961, "inside of me, it was like a bomb, I wanted out." While visiting her husband's sister in New York, Caroline begged the sister for the name of an abortionist. The sister, who is "very religious" refused, but relented when she realized how desperately unhappy and suicidal Caroline was. Caroline went to the abortionist's apartment with the money and lay down on a table while a liquid was inserted with a syringe. By the next day, the pain had become intense, and Caroline "felt like I was going blind." She was rushed to the hospital, where the doctor who treated her told her that the liquid was paint thinner and that she might die. Caroline remained in the hospital for six days. When asked how the experience had affected her, she replied,"Did it change my life? Oh yes. Oh yes. I became a woman."

Like Caroline, Carmen was also desperately unhappy in her relationship with her partner:

> I was young. I already had two kids. One wasn't even two yet, my other one was five months old. I wasn't working. I didn't finish high school. I was going through lots of physical abuse. I was living with the father of my babies. I was pretty naive.

When Carmen discovered she was pregnant again, at age twenty-one, "I didn't really have anybody to talk to. I didn't want to tell my mother. I didn't want to tell my sister. ... Nobody knew." It was 1969 and Carmen knew very little about abortion:

> I knew this girl, and she had gone to a lady, and the lady used, I think, a shower attachment. She used to charge them $50.00, they used to go to this lady.

Carmen did not have $50, but she was resourceful at using the library despite being a high school drop-out:

> So I went to the library and I took out a book on abortion. I found out from the lady who had gone for the abortion that the abortionist would stick the tube through the uterus, so I started reading about abortion and figured out how to do it. I was trying to figure out what would be the safest thing to use to do it, to stick something through there. ... I used a toothbrush. It was painful.

That night, Carmen began chilling and bleeding and was taken to the hospital, where the doctor performed a D and C and wrote it up as a miscarriage.

Both Carolyn and Carmen were able to make new lives for themselves. Carolyn works for a social service agency. Carmen completed her G.E.D. and several years of college and works in a neighborhood health clinic.

For each of these women, deciding to get an abortion involved a consideration of herself as a woman, herself within a relationship, or both. In the next chapter, I will describe women's beliefs about gender relationships, how these beliefs fit (or didn't fit) their experiences, and how those beliefs might have changed.

3

Experiences and Beliefs About Relationships

A major portion of each interview was devoted to a discussion of relationships, including each woman's experience with one or more relationships, her beliefs about relationships, and how she positioned herself within a male dominant culture. Five women, talking about their children, characterized the continuation of these pregnancies as choices, based, in part, on the relationship that existed at the time. Eight women had more than one abortion, and these choices were also related to the relationship. Ten of the twenty women described at least one relationship that involved abuse. One (Sylvia) was in a relationship that was emotionally abusive at the time of the interview.

Male Control vs. Egalitarian Relationships

Several women made a point of describing Puerto Rican cultural norms about male dominance to me, an "Americana" researcher, who presumably did not know much about Puerto Rican men. Julia, for example, told me about her upcoming marriage to the father of two of her six children, the man she had lived with for five years:

> We're going to get married in May, which I don't want to but I have to. [Why not?] I never want to get married, but he says we should for the kids. It took five years for him to brainwash me, for the kids. I want to be with him but I don't want to get married. I don't want a man telling me what to do. You know when you get legally married, your man thinks he owns you. [Do you think he will do this?] I know men do that. Puerto Rican men, I *know*. You're my wife and you have to do this.

Describing the events leading to her divorce, Marisol explained that her husband lost his job and she had to work. She continued, first in general terms about Puerto Rican men, and then about her own husband:

Puerto Rican men have tempers. As long as they feel they're in control, they're okay, but if they lose control, they become pretty violent, and he had never got started. Women in my family have been abused, threatened, and I knew I wouldn't stand for it. Even though he had a temper, and I knew he was capable of hurting me or my children, he never did, in those fourteen years. But there was always the threat that if I spoke up as a person, that he would just knock me down, because he is the man and I am the woman. And I was right because when he went back to work, after having him home and being so supportive because he would not look for a job, I thought I had a right to speak, and he didn't believe I did, and he became abusive, and the marriage ended, because he had raped me.

Marisol described the marriage as a good one until the balance of power began to shift in her favor.

In order to gain some measure of these women's beliefs about gender, and to elicit discussion about relationships, jobs, and children, I asked each of them the four agree/disagree questions from the General Social Survey which were designed to test attitudes about the "traditional" division of labor between husbands and wives (Mason and Lu 1988). These questions are: (1) It is much better for everyone if the man is the achiever and the woman takes care of the home and family. (2) It is more important for a wife to help her husband's career than to have one herself. (3) A working mother can establish just as warm and secure a relationship with her children as a mother who does not work. (4) A preschool child is likely to suffer if his or her mother works. Mason and Lu give the percentages of women's profeminist responses, in 1985, for each of the four questions as 53.4%, 62.4%, 67.3% and 53.1% (p. 45). They do not provide breakdowns on completely profeminist or antifeminist responses, or combinations of responses.

Twelve women, or 60% gave profeminist answers to every question, seventeen, or 85% gave profeminist answers to the first two questions, about jobs, two gave antifeminist answers, and one was ambivalent ("it depends"). They indicated more disagreement about the effects of a mother's employment on her children. Five women who gave profeminist answers about women's employment gave antifeminist answers to one or more of the questions about children.

Julia, who has six children, thinks that children "need their love first," and that mothers should wait until their children are three or four years old, "and know they have love" before they take a job. Cherrie, who left an abusive relationship and raised her daughter alone, explained that

I had to work all my life because I was a single mother. How many things I missed, because I had to work to survive in this city. I didn't

know the language. I didn't have anyone to counsel me. I was feeling
guilty, that I didn't stay with my daughter.

Cherrie's reaction to these questions suggests what other women
state more explicitly, namely that resources, or, more commonly, lack of
resources, are an important determinant of how women experience their
employment and their childrens' welfare. Evelyn, who has no children,
is college educated and politically articulate. She said that when she
was growing up, she thought she would have about six children, but
now she has doubts about raising

> even two kids, because it's too hard. This society has made it so difficult
> for people to live. I realize why there are so many homeless people.
> You have to pay rent, phone, gas, heat, water, car. I'm struggling [to
> pay these] with all this education behind me. [This society is] geared to
> an individual mentality. Too bad if you don't have a support system, or
> a wealthy family, *too bad* — and that's the mentality of America, the
> haves and the have nots. I consider myself poor. I live okay, but I live
> from check to check.

Both Cherrie's and Evelyns's comments suggest the importance of
class (as well as gender) as a factor in how these women responded to
questions about employment and childrearing. The questions suggest
that the "traditional" division of labor is the norm, and the purpose of
the questions is to gauge attitudes about deviation from that norm. The
wording of the survey questions assume a middle class orientation, especially with employment referred to as a "career," or "achievement." I
altered the wording of question two to "career or job."

Most employed Puerto Ricans, male and female, work in service or
manufacturing jobs at relatively low wages, and with little job security
(Gilbang and Falcon 1993). Additionally, 1990 census figures indicate
that 43.3% of Puerto Rican families were single-mother families, a larger
percentage than other Latina groups, and a larger percentage than the
population as a whole (Gilbarg and Falcon 1993: 72). Given this situation, beliefs about employment may be related to economic survival as
well as to gender roles. Nevertheless, the additional comments of some
women suggest the importance of beliefs about gender in their responses. Two, Miriam and Lupe, defined themselves as feminists.
Lupe's response to each of the first two questions was "hell no."

Felice, a widow, said that during her marriage she put her husband's
job first, but that she has since changed her thinking. At age fifteen,
Lucy began a relationship with the father of three of her four boys, who
is nine years older than she is. She described the relationship this way:

He wanted things his way. I felt like a father-daughter type relationship. He didn't want me to go out. I couldn't go out unless I was with him. He wouldn't take me to the movies. I was always home. When I had to go to school, he was taking me and picking me up, right by the door.

It took Lucy "a long time" to persuade him to let her get her G.E.D. His response to her wanting to do this was, "you're a woman, you should be in the house." Lucy is no longer in a relationship with this man and summed up her thinking about the four attitude questions:

I think both parents should be able to work and have a relationship with their children. I don't think a pre-school child would suffer if his mom is not there. I had one of my kids in a pre-school and he was just fine. In kindergarten, he was one of the best students in his class. I really think that both parents should have a career, and both parents should work together. They should be able to support each other in the decisions they make. Let's say she wants to go to school, one should be able to stay with the kids and one should go to school. You know, alternate, ... both of them spend time with the kids."

Carmen, who had an abortion as part of her escape from a violent relationship, gave the harshest analysis of the effect of male dominance on the woman:

A woman should have her own life, if she wants to work. The way I look at it, in the neighborhood, women who are at home, who are not working, take their kids to school in the morning and pick them up at school. They just do that, like it's a job, a duty. They don't really talk to their kids. I see them going a lot. It's like they have no life of their own. Their life is taking the kids to school, waiting for their husbands, cooking for them. It's like a duty. [Some of them] become so miserable they end up abusing their kids.

Perhaps a more important determinant than female employment of equality within a relationship is that the relationship is characterized by sharing rather than male control. Many women spoke, resentfully, of previous relationships they characterized as dominating or abusive.

Mayra, for example, said that she was about to leave her husband when she discovered she was pregnant. She decided to continue that pregnancy because she had not yet had a child and decided that she wanted to. She said of her daughter, "I chose to have her, definitely," although her concern was "would I have even more difficulty getting out of my marriage." Mayra described her thinking when she got pregnant again, in another relationship:

I had come out of this stormy, suffocating, subservient relationship, at the tail end of nursing a child. I had made a three hundred sixty degree turn as far as my self-entitlement as a person. Because of it, I was prepared to do what I needed to do.

She explained how deciding to get an abortion changed her:

It confirmed all of those different stages I had gone through, spiritually, emotionally, and intellectually in my life. I was now living my life the way I felt I wanted to, and when I made the decision to have that abortion, it confirmed that my life belonged to me.

Mayra described her relationship with Daniel as more "serious" than her relationship with her former husband in that the relationship with her husband was merely physical, while she and Daniel shared "a bond," intellectually and emotionally: "Daniel was something I needed to happen. It restored my faith in men, and relationships."

Surviving an Abusive Relationship

According to the Federal Bureau of Investigation, "forty-one percent of all American wives are beaten by their husbands at least once during their married lives" (Chicago Abused Women Coalition n.d.). Male violence or abuse of a female partner cuts across lines of class, race, and ethnicity. According to the Illinois Coalition Against Domestic Violence (undated) the "Chicago police receive more calls to help resolve family violence than calls for all other serious crimes -- murder, rape, aggravated assault -- *combined*" (emphasis in original).

In her booklet about sexual assault and domestic violence, Catherine Walters (1984) states that "[b]oth domestic violence and sexual assault have a long history as acceptable behavior toward women" (2). She goes on to explain that

the overwhelming fact is that violence against women has happened since nearly the beginning of recorded history. It occurs under every imaginable circumstance and it continues to happen daily to women of all races and classes, in all walks of life. Women are logically the victims of male aggression because we live in a society where we are taught that men are and should be superior to women in every way. This belief in male superiority gives men the 'right' to exercise control over women in the forms they choose. Women may be assaulted or abused not as individual persons, but for what they represent. Violence toward women is most appropriately viewed as the historical and current expression of male dominance (3).

Given the pervasiveness of men's use of violence to control women it is not surprising that violence was a common theme in the narratives of these Puerto Rican women. Ten related abusive relationships or incidents of abuse. Of these ten, five said the abuse was related to their decision to get an abortion. Caroline, Carmen, Sylvia, and Ana's accounts are in chapter two. The fifth woman, Julia, was just shy of her fifteenth birthday and already had one child, when she discovered she was pregnant again. After her abortion, she told her boyfriend she had miscarried, but he figured out the truth, and then, "he hit me. We got into a fight and we left each other." Of the ten accounts of abuse, five were not directly related to the abortion, and the women (Marisol, Mercedes, Helena, Cherrie, and Gloria) are no longer in these relationships.

Even from this small number of interviews it appears that male violence is related to the woman's vulnerability. Eight women indicated that they married or began a live-in relationship in order to leave a very strict home or because they were pregnant. Of these eight, six experienced violence at the hands of that male partner. Of the twelve women who did not "have" to marry or move in with a man, four recounted incidents of violence and eight did not.

Mercedes' experience provides an example of the cumulative nature of vulnerability to violence and emotional manipulation. She became pregnant at age sixteen by a man who became abusive, so she returned, with her infant son, to her family of origin. She began seeing another man.

> It was my second pregnancy. [I was] dating a guy, he was going out with someone else, my family didn't like him, and I came out pregnant. I loved him and wanted to keep the baby because of that, but I didn't want to keep it because of my family. My family didn't like him because he wanted to be with both of us. I was so in love with him because I had been through a relationship with my older son's father. He was abusive, and I was scared to get pregnant again. He comforted me. He was there for me. I was in love with him.

The man continued his relationship with both Mercedes and the other woman. In fact, the other woman was pregnant by him when he began seeing Mercedes. He expected Mercedes to have the baby. He said, "things were going to change," but in addition to being involved in another relationship, "he was going to court -- and what if he went to jail?" Mercedes continued

> I told the man to help me think what to do and he said 'have it, have it' and then he said if you don't want to have it, he would pay for it. I asked him would it change our relationship and he said no, it wouldn't change anything. The night before, we stood together, and I was going

to do it, and he kept saying nothing's going to change. I was undecided because I did want the baby. I cared for him so much, but due to the circumstances [of the other woman and the possibility of his going to jail], I didn't want to be left alone. [My son's father wasn't there] and that's what I was scared of again.

After Mercedes had the abortion things did change, for the worse:

but him, he lied. He acted all different, he kept telling me that it could have been his son, and every time it came up, he said 'you killed it' and I said 'well, you gave me the money and you stood there and waited for me,' but he blamed everything on me. ... Every time I would see baby stuff I would start crying.

When she got pregnant by this man a second time, about a year later, she continued this pregnancy and had a son. Three months into the pregnancy, the partner left. Mercedes now lives with another man and her two sons. She said her new partner "treats me good, and treats my kids good."

Evaluating the Relationship in the Context of an Unplanned Pregnancy

In the course of their narratives eleven women talked about other abortions they had had, pregnancies they considered ending but continued, or both. Six had more than one abortion, three continued pregnancies they had considered terminating, and two did both.

Carmen, whose experience with an illegal abortion is described in the previous chapter, was in another relationship several years later. She was working on her G.E.D. and her life was "more together." When she discovered she was pregnant, she "thought about the previous time. At that time, I felt more stable, so I decided to have the baby. If I had been as miserable as last time, I would have done it again."

In fact, she did do it again, in 1976. She had been in an accident and needed x-rays taken. She was taking birth control pills and did not know she was pregnant. One reason she ended that pregnancy was her concern about damage to the fetus from the x-ray.

Mayra has two children, and with each pregnancy she considered whether or not to continue or terminate it. Her first pregnancy is discussed earlier in this chapter. She became pregnant with her second child before she and her present husband were married. The relationship seemed stable and they were planning marriage, so Mayra continued this pregnancy.

These women's brief accounts of other abortions did not suggest meanings other that those discussed in the previous chapter. However, some accounts of pregnancies in which a conscious decision was made to have the baby indicate the importance of women's perceptions of the quality of their relationships. Mayra's account of her pregnancy by her present husband is one example. The most striking example is that of Lucy. She was twenty-six at the time of the interview, and described the abortion she had at the age of eighteen, when she already had one child. About halfway through the interview, in response to a question about what she hoped to be doing within the next few years, she said she wanted "to have my four boys in Catholic school." I was surprised by this sudden revelation of three other children and asked her to tell me about them. She said that, subsequent to the abortion, she and her oldest son's father had gotten back together. She had each of the two boys because she was with this partner, and said that "if I had been alone, I wouldn't have been able to." Her youngest son is by another partner whom she is still with. In response to a question about what she might tell a friend who came to her for advice about deciding how to resolve an unplanned pregnancy, she described a situation in which she actually did advise a friend:

> It's only your decision. I went through it. If you're not ready, don't have it. If he's going to be there with you, willing to support you, willing to marry you, then go ahead. Don't be left alone with a child. I guess she talked to him. They're together and they did have a little girl.

In my earlier (1990) study of fifteen white women who got abortions during the spring of 1989 at a Chicago area clinic, I determined that five of the fifteen women used the abortion decision to nurture the relationship. They generally believed the relationship would be harmed by "having to get married" or "trapping" the man. Charlene and Christie are two examples from this study.

When Charlene discovered her pregnancy her life was "kind of in between." She was working in a nursing home, preparing to take her G.E.D. exam, and "working on the relationship" with her boyfriend. They had been dating casually for a few months but Charlene sensed that it could become serious. She did not tell him about the pregnancy because she had good reason to believe that if she did, he would offer to marry her and expect her to have the baby. She did not believe this was a good basis for marriage. He might come to resent being "trapped." Her own parents had fought a lot and finally divorced and Charlene hopes to have a more secure marriage. She and her boyfriend are now living together. She describes the relationship as "much stronger" and says that they are planning marriage.

Christie had been seeing her boyfriend for about a year when she discovered she was pregnant. The decision to get the abortion was a mutual one and she told no one else.

> [He] said if I wanted him to, that he would marry me, ... but we just agreed that I couldn't have the baby ... I thought I was too young, and he's too young. I definitely wasn't ready to get married and neither was he. ... I care what he feels. It was his child too.

Christie thinks the relationship is stronger. At the time of the interview they were planning to live together and were considering marriage.

The parents of Charlene and Christie are divorced. Both women stated that their parents' divorce has caused them to take their own relationships very seriously. They reject the idea of "having" to get married, both for the sake of the marriage relationship and for its negative effect on the child. None of the Puerto Rican respondents said that having to get married might have a negative effect on the relationship or the child.

An informant interview with Inez, a counselor at a Chicago abortion clinic, contributes to an understanding of this cultural difference between Puerto Rican and white women. Inez lives in an area of Chicago that was generally Puerto Rican and is now undergoing gentrification. She associates in her job, in her neighborhood, and in her friendships, with both Puerto Ricans and Anglos, and contrasted their outlooks on relationships by describing their comments about her marriage. Inez married at age twenty-two, and she and her husband do not have children. According to Inez, virtually all her Anglo friends think twenty-two is much too young to get married, and her Puerto Rican friends wonder why she waited so long. As Inez becomes acquainted with her Puerto Rican neighbors, they ask if she is married. When she says yes, and then says that she has no children, they express surprise that Inez and her husband got married without having to legitimate a pregnancy.

These women, in general, value committed relationships and resist male dominance. Often, a decision about how to resolve an unplanned pregnancy depends on the woman's assessment of the quality of the relationship and its stability. Sometimes, resisting male dominance or male violence involves acting in ways that are inconsistent with her upbringing. Strategies for coping with this inconsistency are the subject of the next chapter.

4

Cultural Stories and Collective Stories

The focus of this chapter is on what Laurel Richardson (1990) terms the "cultural story" of Puerto Rican women. According to Richardson, a cultural story is about the "normative order" (128). For many Puerto Rican women, the cultural story is about virginity, family, motherhood, and male dominance. It includes the idea that contraception and abortion are wrong (Burgos and Diaz Perez 1986; Campbell 1984). In contrast to the cultural story, the collective story is an alternative one. It is about self-determination and resisting male control. While the main focus of this chapter is on the cultural story, as some women relate their responses to the cultural story, they begin the collective story.

Judith Ortiz Cofer (1990) provides a description of how the traditional Puerto Rican cultural story worked in her own life. In her remembrance of her girlhood spent alternately in Puerto Rico and Paterson, New Jersey, Cofer shows how what it means to be a good Puerto Rican woman is communicated by strict rules of behavior and by the elaborate stories older women family members tell to younger ones. She describes the oral tradition this way:

> At three or four o'clock in the afternoon, the hour of cafe con leche, the women of my family gathered in Mama's living room to speak of important things, and to tell stories for the hundredth time, as if to each other, meant to be overheard by us young girls, their daughters. ... They told real-life stories, though as I later learned, always embellishing them with a little or a lot of dramatic detail, and they told *cuentos*, the morality and cautionary tales told by the women in our family for generations (14,15).

Cofer's description of the oral tradition shows how this tradition maintains the interdependence of family members, and the respect for one's elders that characterize Puerto Rican family life. As Cofer described the cultural story she learned from her mother and other family members, consistent themes were virginity, family, and motherhood as central to women's lives. Virginity until marriage is extremely important and parents enforce strict rules of behavior for girls with this goal in mind. There is no place in this story for abortion. The availability of abortion would undercut two tenets of the cultural story. One is that non-marital sex is a transgression that must be paid for, and another is that motherhood is the core of female identity.

Focus Groups: Experiencing and Resisting the Cultural Story

One purpose of the focus group interviews was to gain some insight into the "cultural story" the participants grew up with, and how their life experiences might have changed their beliefs and their behavior. The responses of the older focus group participants resonate with themes similar to Cofer's. This group of six Puerto Rican women staff a pre-school program in a neighborhood church and the group interview took place over lunch, on a day when the children were absent. Responding to a question about what they learned while growing up about being a good Puerto Rican woman, they emphasized respecting their parents, virginity, and strict rules designed to keep them close to home. Nina's response is typical:

> Respect your parents. No sex until you get married. I didn't even know about it. My mother didn't tell me anything."

Another participant, Luz, described her girlhood this way:

> My mother was strict. I couldn't go anywhere. I lived on Fairfield Avenue. The next street was Chicago Avenue, where the stores were, and people used to say what they got on Chicago Avenue, and I pretended I knew what they were talking about.

Madeline told about talking to boys from inside the window of her apartment, and having to shut the window abruptly if her father walked into the room.

Becoming pregnant as an unmarried teenager is, of course, a serious violation of one's upbringing. Additionally, the norm of respecting one's parents by not openly violating rules (Friedman 1991) makes revealing a pregnancy especially difficult. As Carmen put it, "just saying 'Mom, I'm pregnant' is like losing respect."

Delia's description of how she let her family know she was pregnant at age sixteen provides a dramatic illustration of pregnancy as a violation of one's upbringing, revealing a pregnancy as showing a lack of respect, and family interdependence. Delia told her sister first. The night they told their mother they were so immobilized by fear that they delayed until 3:00 a.m. and woke their mother up. They had each packed a suitcase full of belongings and put them in the car:

> We were going to go to my cousin's house if mother, if she started hitting me or kicked me out. We had our gym shoes on. We were ready to run out. My sister said, 'if she starts hitting you, run.'

When the girls woke their mother up and told her Delia was pregnant, she began to cry, and said that she would tell their father in the morning. Then she said, "If he kicks you out, I'll go with you. You're my baby. I'm going to go with you."

Delia's father didn't kick her out. He cried too, and wouldn't speak to Delia for several days. Eventually, Delia's family accepted the pregnancy and welcomed the baby, although at first she was "the talk of the family, and I have a big family."

Delia's mother did not indicate that she could have challenged her husband's authority if he had ordered his pregnant daughter to leave home, yet she stated her intention not to abandon her. Delia's arrangements with her sister and their cousin, and her mother's promise to Delia, are examples of generational and female bonding as a strategy for coping with parental and male authority. The fact that Delia and her sister made plans to run away to a cousin's house, rather than a friend's house is an indication of family interdependence.

Questions about male behavior elicited resentment of male dominance. According to Nina, Puerto Rican men are proud, demanding, and jealous, as well as sensitive and lovable. Roberta explained that Puerto Rican men are "okay at first, but a few months into the relationship, they try to control you, bossing you around, and then you got to lay the cards on them." Nina thinks male-female relationships have changed since her mother's generation, in that "Puerto Rican women are not taking this *machismo* -- we woke up." There was general agreement with Luz's definition of an ideal relationship as "close friendship" characterized by "trust."

The twelve younger focus group participants (ages 18-21) attend an alternative high school for students who have dropped out of public school. Virtually all of them are from homes at or below the poverty line. Only three live with both parents. The rest live with their mother, mother and stepfather, grandparents, or a boyfriend. Remaining a virgin until marriage was not brought up as an issue in this group. None was married, and six were mothers. The major topic of discussion was male dominance and how to cope with it.

In response to the question about what they learned while growing up about being a good Puerto Rican woman, Marisa replied:

> The way I was brought up was, the man has to be king of the house.
> You should have the bath water running when he comes home from
> work, [and] the food already cooked.

In contrast, Lucy's mother raised her to believe that "women can take
care of everything." Lucy described her mother's relationships with
men: "If they want to be 'man of the house' my mom would refuse. I've
learned to be that way too." Nevertheless, Lucy describes her stepfather's treatment of her as very strict. He wanted her to "come home
early --leave at 7:00, be home at 8:30."

The most animated discussion centered around attempts by their
boyfriends to control their behavior. According to Liz: "You only can
talk to them. You can't talk to their friends. You gotta stay in the
house." Maria added, "they want you to be like their figure mother
[cooking and cleaning]." Lucy explained that a boyfriend will try to
control his girlfriend when the relationship becomes serious, and he
thinks of her as "his lady."

There was general agreement with Sylvia's strategy for dealing with
male dominance:

> You tell him 'no.' He tells you to cook. Then you want to wear some-
> thing to go out, he says 'no.' You say, 'why not, you're not my father,
> you're not my mother.' In the beginning of the relationship, a girl
> should put a stop to all that. That's what I did, and he's not like that at
> all with me.

Their agreement on the characteristics of a good relationship echoed
that of the older focus group: "trust," "honesty," "communication,"
"not doing all the work [cooking]," and "being able to go out." When
asked if relationships like this were common, they replied, "not really."

The cultural story of virginity, motherhood, and male dominance is,
of course, not unique to Puerto Rican women. Variants of it are shared
by women with a Catholic or evangelical Protestant background. It is
undercut, in every culture where these exist, by the availability of legal
abortion and contraception. This separation of sex from reproduction
makes possible a new story about being female.

Religion and the Cultural Story

Most Puerto Ricans who practice a religion are Catholic, and Pentecostals also have a substantial Puerto Rican membership. Both of these
denominations are strongly opposed to abortion under any circumstances, and the Catholic church is opposed to contraception other than
periodic abstinence. This sets a conflict for a Puerto Rican woman be-

tween her own (and perhaps her family's) needs and the demands of her church.

The Catholic church may have less direct influence on the behavior of Puerto Rican women than common stereotypes about Latinas suggest. Puerto Ricans who label themselves Catholic often have weak institutional ties and may attend mass rarely or not at all (Badillo 1992). According to Nydia Garcia-Preto (1982), "[m]ost Puerto Ricans have some distrust of organized religion, the Church, and the priest, and believe they can make contact with God and the supernatural without clergy" (169). During a lunch conversation with two health care workers who were raised Catholic in Puerto Rico and now attend a Lutheran church in Humboldt Park, one of them assured me, based on her experiences at worship, that "Lutheran is the same as Catholic -- except the priests get married." An older (age 59) member of the Head Start staff group who came in near the end of the focus group summed up the changes she has observed in the reproductive behavior of Latinas as follows:

> through the years I've worked with parents of Head Start. I remember the first year, I had mothers with seven or eight children, many children. I would say about five years ago, one or two children. I'm talking about Latino. I used to hear discussions among the parents: 'Are you going to have any more children? The Father is not going to give communion to you if he knows you are using contraception.' And the answer was, 'Is he going to support my children?' So they don't care anymore what any priest says. They have formed their own consciences and have decided what is the best.

Nevertheless, traditional Puerto Rican culture values motherhood as the core of female identity. There is a generalized belief that "God will provide." For example, a common Latina saying is, *"donde come uno, comen dos,* where you can feed one, you can feed two" (Giachello and Torres 1991; informant interview with a health care worker). Several informant interviewees suggested that one reason Puerto Rican women do not share the fact of an unplanned pregnancy is their belief that others will try to talk them out of having an abortion.

None of the women I interviewed was raised or is a practicing Pentecostal. I have no way of knowing whether this reflects their smaller numbers within the Puerto Rican population or an acceptance of Pentecostal teachings against abortion. It may be that Puerto Rican Pentecostals are even more secretive about abortion than other Puerto Rican women. A brief conversation with Irene, a Puerto Rican Pentecostal woman who has adult children indicates how actively her church is involved in its members' lives. Irene's English is limited and I do not speak Spanish at all, so it took several minutes before she understood what my research was about. When she realized that I wanted to interview women who had had abortions, she replied, "Oh no. I can't help with that. I would stand in the way of someone to take the baby out." She went on to relate how, that very evening, there was to be a baby shower at her church. Irene had told this young pregnant woman to make a list of all the things she needed so that church members could buy them and bring them to the shower. Irene told me that she does not believe in abortion because "I am a Christian," and that if I were to meet anyone who is pregnant and needs money to call her. While some women might welcome this generosity, the assumption underlying it is that the only reason a woman might not want to have a baby is because she cannot afford to raise it. There is no room in this world view for a woman who does not want to have a baby because she wants to continue her education, or leave a relationship. The practices of Irene and other members of her church indicate the sacrifices they are willing to make to enforce the idea that motherhood is the core of female identity.

In her study of California women who were activists on either side of the abortion controversy, Kristin Luker (1984) discovered that, for each group of women, the underlying issue determining their beliefs about abortion was their belief about the place and meaning of motherhood in women's lives. In general, anti-abortion women accepted a definition of motherhood as a basic condition of being female. The idea of planning children -- rationally integrating childrearing into one's life -- was incomprehensible to them. Pro-choice women, on the other hand, conceptualized motherhood as a freely chosen relationship, integrated into a life that might include other possibilities. Luker concluded from her study that abortion "is a referendum on the place and meaning of motherhood" (193). Since Luker does not mention ethnicity it is reasonable to assume that most of the women she interviewed are white. Nevertheless, her insight that beliefs about female identity and motherhood underlie beliefs about abortion is important. One theme that recurs in Puerto Rican women's narratives is resistance to the idea of motherhood as a woman's sole identity.

While Puerto Rican women may believe that their own needs are important, they often do not have the cultural warrant to choose abortion that is part of mainstream American culture. They may not perceive the ideas expressed by the pro-choice movement as relevant to them. Additionally, Puerto Rican women do not share the mainstream cultural norm of personal autonomy within the family. Instead, the Puerto Rican cultural norm is one of family interdependence (Friedman 1992). All this makes the need to keep the abortion secret especially difficult. Lacking both cultural and personal support for the abortion decision, many Puerto Rican women face it alone.

Puerto Rican Teenagers and Peer Culture

Puerto Rican women living in the United States are influenced by Puerto Rican culture in general and by the neighborhood culture that exists wherever they live. Focus group participants talked about their socialization by family members and they discussed Puerto Rican culture in general. This section presents a variant of the cultural story, one transmitted to young women by their neighborhood peers. Human subjects protocol prevented me from interviewing minors. This version of the cultural story is presented through informant interviews with four health care providers and social workers who work primarily with Puerto Rican teenagers in Humboldt Park, West Town, or Logan Square.

For teenagers growing up in a low income neighborhood, peer pressure and other neighborhood conditions usually override parental attempts to control their behavior. Jonathan Crane (1991) shows that the probability that an individual will engage in problematic behavior, in this case teen pregnancy, jumps at the bottom of the distribution of neighborhood quality. In other words, very poor neighborhoods experience almost uncontrollable epidemics of problems such as drugs, gang violence, teenage pregnancy and teenage childbearing. The mechanism of the neighborhood effect is peer influence. As applied to teen pregnancy and childbearing, it suggests that teenagers in very poor neighborhoods get pregnant at an early age because many of their friends are getting pregnant and having babies, and this behavior spreads by contagion. The interviews with health care providers and social workers indicate how peer influence works.

Neighborhood effects through peer pressure are clearly evident to Eva in the work she does with Puerto Rican teenagers in two low income high schools in Chicago as an advocate for teenage mothers. Eva works with students from two public high schools, Wells and Kelvin, helping these students locate such resources as day care, tutoring, prenatal care, and public aid. The student body at Wells Academy is about 50% Latino, 50% African American, and 80% low income, serving students from West Town and the Cabrini Green public housing development. Kelvin High School has the highest concentration of Latino students in the city (98%) and about 60% of the students are low income.

According to Eva, pregnancy is "common" at both schools. These girls have low self-esteem and are not involved in the school. Virtually all her girls are from single parent homes, and they get pregnant "because there is nothing else to do." Girls often act as if the baby were a "toy" and they enjoy showing the baby off. Especially at Wells Academy, the poorer of the two schools, pregnancy "spreads life wildfire."

Both high schools have instituted a rule forbidding students from bringing babies to school, an implicit aknowledgment of the contagion effect. Eva discovered this rule when she went to Kelvin to make a presentation about parenthood to a class. She brought four young mothers with her, and the mothers brought their babies. Eva was summoned to the principal's office and informed of the rule. She was told that when the girls bring their babies to school, pregnancy "spreads like wildfire." She was also told that the official reason for the rule is compliance with the fire code. Girls at Kelvin High School sometimes violate this rule, claiming they cannot find a babysitter. The girls are sent home. There is no day care at Kelvin High School.

One pattern described by Eva is a disturbing variant of Anderson's (1990) finding, from his ethnographic study of Philadelphia teenagers, that a girl derives status from the identity of the male she got pregnant with. According to Eva, about one third of her case load involves young girls of about fifteen who get pregnant by gang members who are much older, over twenty. These young girls "flaunt" their pregnancies, enjoying the high status of carrying this particular gang member's baby. Toward the end of the pregnancy the man loses interest in the girl and ends the relationship, sometimes violently, by beating her up. Eva believes that most of the young girls in a relationship with an older gang member experience violence throughout the relationship, and about half the girls admit this to her. The girls accept the violence as normal and "they take it so naturally ... it's part of being his girlfriend." A typical comment is "he beat me up last Friday night, then we made up, and he took me out on Saturday night."

Pronatalist pressure comes from the boys as well as the girls. Boys, in general, do not like the idea of birth control and are very much against abortion. "She's not going to get rid of *my* baby" is a typical sentiment. Young teenage girls know virtually nothing about birth control and nothing about dating either. The boy controls the date, and it never occurs to girls of about fifteen that they have any say in whether or not to have sex. Eva observes that some of the older girls realize that they do have a say about both sex and birth control.

In general, knowledge about birth control and access to it are limited. One good source is the Erie Teen Center, near Wells Academy. The staff at this center explain options in language the teenagers understand. In Eva's experience, teens who learn about birth control from this center are more apt to use it than teens who learn about birth control from sources not geared to teenagers. Nevertheless, it seems that few young Puerto Rican women use contraceptives.

My research took place in 1991 and 1992, during an anti-abortion presidential administration with a stated policy of not providing public funding to any agency that even mentioned to a woman with a problem pregnancy that abortion is an option. Although this policy was never enforced, it was found constitutional by the U.S. Supreme Court (*Rust v. Sullivan*) in 1991, and would have been enforced had George Bush been re-elected in 1992. Even though my research involved women who had already had abortions, staff of agencies receiving public funds often seemed to be leery of working with me. Through mutual friends, I was able to interview a doctor, Madeline, who worked at the Erie Teen Health Center. She described her patients as poor, working poor, and single parents. Her belief that "pregnancy is a contagious disease" echoes Eva's observation. Madeline believes that some girls "get pregnant almost on purpose. They don't use birth control. They are stuck in homes that are broken. With a kid, they can get on public aid and move out of the house." Although some girls come to Erie for birth control so they can finish high school or go to college, these girls are the exception. Madeline estimates that only 20-25% of her patients come in for birth control and of these, most already have a child, and the reality of caring for a child has set in. In her five years at Erie, Madeline has seen "several thousand" patients, and only two or three of them requested any kind of contraception prior to becoming sexually active. Madeline stated that most of her patients are against abortion. "I couldn't do that," is a typical response.

In addition to their avoidance of birth control, Madeline described two other general characteristics of these teenagers: (1) the "infallible youth syndrome" of "denial," either that they will engage in sexual activity or that they will, as a result of sexual activity, get pregnant; and (2) a presentation of themselves as "forced" into sexual activity for the partner's sake, out of love for him.

Lisa is a social worker at Roberto Clemente High School. Her observations are consistent with Eva's and Madeline's. In Lisa's experience, very few teens use contraception. Girls are "afraid" to take the pill and boys refuse to use condoms. Virtually all unplanned pregnancies are carried to term and the girls raise the babies. Typical sentiments are "it's unplanned but I want to keep it," and "I don't want to kill my baby." Some girls hope the baby will be "someone to talk to me." Lisa brings up the option of abortion with girls who discuss their unplanned pregnancies with her, but they almost always reject it.

According to Lisa, pregnant girls are in the mainstream at Clemente. In an effort to help these girls continue their education, Clemente provides resources to pregnant and parenting teens such as health care and child care and referrals. WIC and public aid offices are located at the school. Lisa's impression is that about 40% of the girls return to high school after a birth, and another 25-30% return the following year. Some girls remain with their family of origin, and parents provide support for their daughter and her baby.

Eva provided a more elaborate description of parental support, consistent with Lisa's. She described a typical pattern in the Latino community whereby the boy's family takes in the young mother and the baby. This reflects the belief that it is the male's responsibility to provide for his girlfriend and their child. Since he is too young to provide adequately, his parent(s) take on this role. During Eva's own youth, five of her brothers brought their girlfriends home to live with them. A girl in this situation drops out of school and takes on a role like that of a dependent wife. The relationship usually ends after a few months and the girl returns to her family of origin. It is at this point that she realizes that she will probably have to support herself, tries to get back into school, and comes to Eva for help. Eva believes that family support at this time is critical to successful outcomes. One factor that has an effect on family support, in Eva's experience, is religion. A Catholic or Protestant mother will encourage her own pregnant daughter to remain at home with her, and will provide emotional and financial support to the young mother and baby. She may also allow the boyfriend to live with them if necessary. When I described this pattern to Lisa, she agreed that it is typical, and stated that both Catholic and Protestant parents are more likely to provide support for their daughters than those who do not practice a religion.

Most informants simply described teenage abortions as "rare." Only one, Luz, a mental health counselor, described a pattern for these abortions. In her experience, a young girl is often brought in by her mother. The girl wants the abortion because the boy has a new girlfriend, or either one (or both) of the teens is using drugs. The pregnancy and the abortion are generally kept secret from the girl's father.

In these four accounts, as well as in the focus group composed of teenagers and young women, virginity is not an issue. The fact of sexual activity is a given. As the norm of virginity breaks down, a new norm about sexual virtue appears to have replaced it. Ruth Horowitz's (1983) ethnographic study of a Mexican-American neighborhood in Chicago provides an analysis of this. Horowitz found the norm of virginity being replaced by what she terms "bounded sexuality." A woman who is not a virgin can claim respectability if she submitted to sex out of love for her partner rather than her own desire, and if she does not use contraception. Unwed pregnancy, having the baby, and being a devoted mother indicate bounded sexuality and confirm that the woman is sexually respectable. For a woman to use contraception indicates that she has planned for sexual activity to occur. This defines her as wanton and her sexuality as "unbound."

Horowitz's analysis of bounded sexuality is consistent with teenagers' and young women's general rejection of contraception and abortion and their insistence on keeping and raising the baby and being a good mother. The pattern Luz described, whereby a girl gets an abortion because the partner has abandoned her or because one of both of them is on drugs, is one in which the idea of bounded sexuality is irrelevant. Although bounded sexuality may have replaced virginity as a norm of sexual virtue, pronatalist values and the idea that motherhood is the core of female identity remain firmly in place.

Puerto Ricans and Abortion: A View from Inside the Abortion Clinic

Two Puerto Rican women who granted me informant interviews are counselors at abortion clinics. In my interview with Marisa, she described her experience of eleven years as a counselor at abortion clinics in Chicago. Over the years, she has counseled many Puerto Ricans. She told me that, in her experience, there are two distinct models of family life for Puerto Ricans, a traditional one and a modern one. According to Marisa there is no middle way; the two are mutually exclusive. Traditional Puerto Ricans are totally against abortion: the sin of sexuality and pregnancy must be punished. Virginity until marriage is extremely important and parents enforce strict behavioral rules for girls with this goal in mind. Marisa told me that her own father insisted she come straight home from school as soon as classes were over and he even got angry with her for looking out the window of their home, wondering aloud if she was looking for boys.

Traditional women do get abortions, however. According to Marisa, about half the Puerto Ricans she sees are traditional. For these women, the experience may involve real isolation. Some come alone, having told no one. With no one to take them home, they must either take a cab home or wait most of the day at the clinic until the anesthetic wears off so they can get home safely. Traditional women almost never come with their husbands because they don't tell their husbands. Some unmarried ones come with boyfriends, however. Marisa described the pattern she encounters this way: the couple comes in for what the woman tells the man is a pregnancy test, though she has made an appointment for an abortion. When Marisa counsels the couple after the test and mentions terminating the pregnancy, the man gets angry, tells his partner and Marisa that abortion is out of the question and that he is taking the woman home. Marisa then takes the woman aside and tells her to call her if she wants to return another day. According to Marisa, these women almost invariably reschedule the abortion and come alone the next time. She speculated that they eventually tell their partners they miscarried.

Puerto Ricans Marisa describes as modern are more accepting of contraception and abortion and are less embarrassed when they talk about abortion. "We're just not ready to have a baby," is typical of what they tell her. Marisa claims that she can tell whether a Puerto Rican male is modern or traditional simply by observing his body language in the waiting room.

Some modern women have traditional origins. Marisa told me that her mother, who lives with her, is traditional, and that she (Marisa) was raised in a traditional way. In her assessment of her experience at the clinic, one's orientation is not a generational phenomenon, i.e. it is not related to age. She speculated that it may be determined by whether or not the woman has a job or other opportunities for contact outside her immediate circle.

Inez is also a counselor at an abortion clinic in Chicago. Her experiences of being between the Puerto Rican and Anglo cultures with respect to the age at which she got married and the fact that she did not get married to legitimate a pregnancy are described in chapter three. Inez is a practicing Catholic. In describing her own upbringing, she said that her mother was stricter than her friends' mothers. She thinks this is because her mother was a single mother and needed to prove herself as a successful parent. Among the values Inez grew up with are virginity and the idea that contraception and abortion are wrong. She added that she was not allowed any contact with boys until she was sixteen. Inez's mother taught her homemaking skills as well, and "by the time I was twelve I knew how to cook a three course meal." Interestingly, another value Inez says she grew up with is the right to be happy. This may explain why she has changed her beliefs about the acceptability of premarital sex, contraception, and abortion. Inez does not think she could ever talk to her mother about an unplanned pregnancy. Her mother knows what Inez's job is, but speaks of it as "just a job," that she wishes Inez would quit. She is not aware of Inez's personal commitment to women's reproductive choice.

Inez told me that she rarely counsels Puerto Rican women because they generally speak English. Her job is to counsel Spanish-speaking patients, most of whom are Mexican. She described these Mexican women as "needy" in that they "need to explain their reasons in great detail." Common reasons are that the husband drinks, they are illegal aliens, and they can't afford to raise another child. These Mexican women are anxious for Inez to understand their reasons for wanting an abortion. Some ask her if she thinks God will punish them. When confronted with this question, Inez tells the woman that she is Catholic and she believes that "God is a forgiving God."

Our discussion of the reasons Mexican women give for having abortions was brief. Nevertheless, it is noteworthy that the reasons Inez gave as the most common are not related to personal goals (e.g. continuing one's education). This is consistent with the findings of Hortensia Amaro's (1982) study of attitudes about abortion among Chicanas in

Los Angeles. Although some of these women had had abortions, their stated reasons for doing so were medical or economic. In contrast, twelve of my Puerto Rican respondents got their abortions in order to maintain their own lives, to "keep on being" who they were. They got abortions because they did not want to sacrifice their educations, jobs, or general well-being. Inez's observations and Amaro's study suggest a possible difference between Mexican and Puerto Rican women that could be explored further.

The Experience of an Illegal Abortion

The right of a woman to terminate a pregnancy may be the most controversial issue in the United States since slavery (Gordon 1986). Much has been written and argued about the circumstances in which a woman should have the choice to abort a pregnancy, and the difficulty of the decision. The religious base of the anti-abortion movement has created the idea, for some, that abortion is a moral dilemma. Many of my respondents spoke of going against their upbringing or their religion. In other words, a woman making a decision about a problem pregnancy might be concerned, or think she should be concerned, about whether or not her decision to abort is moral.

Experiences with illegal abortion are not the focus of this research. Nevertheless, two respondents, Carmen and Caroline, got illegal abortions prior to 1973, and one of my informant interviewees, Rosario, described at great length the beliefs about abortion within her extended family and friends as they existed in the 1940's and 1950's in a predominantly Puerto Rican public housing development in New York City. In all three accounts, the lack of moral ambivalence is striking.

Carolyn and Carmen's abortion narratives are related in chapter two. Each of them is among the ten respondents who said they did not find the abortion decision difficult. Carmen described herself in 1969 as "confused and abused," and added that "sometimes I felt like killing myself, even before I knew I was pregnant." She did not think about morality, but about danger. She explained, "I read about it, that it could be dangerous, and I knew I was taking a chance, that I might kill myself. But I had to find a way." Likewise, Caroline felt her pregnancy was "like a bomb -- I wanted out."

I met Rosario in June of 1992 in Chicago at the annual conference of the National Organization for Women. She is a Puerto Rican who grew up in a predominantly Puerto Rican public housing development in New York City and worked as an emergency room nurse in a large New York public hospital in the early 1960's. I explained my study briefly to her at the conference, and she agreed that I could telephone her a few weeks later for an interview.

Rosario told me that she "cannot think of anyone in my mother's generation who did not get an abortion." She vividly remembers one of her mother's several abortions. Everyone in the family was whispering and saying she would be okay, yet everyone was very upset. Rosario's mother lay in the back room with the shades pulled down until the ambulance arrived. She had lost so much blood that they carried her to the ambulance upside down.

Rosario described her family and immediate circle as practicing Catholics with a "practical" sense of religion. "God would not mind something you needed to do," is a typical expression. Rosario once asked her mother if she thought her abortions "hurt yourself for all eternity," and her mother replied, "no, I had to do it." According to Rosario, many Puerto Rican women worked in the garment factories. Abortion is "what working women did," and it was "necessary to take care of your children." These women self-aborted, paid about twenty-five dollars to a local abortionist, or flew to Puerto Rico for the abortion. Rosario's beliefs about abortion were influenced by the practical Catholicism of her upbringing and by her experiences as an emergency room nurse in New York. As one of the few Spanish-speaking people at the hospital, Rosario was called to assist with Latina patients even during her training. She estimated that she saw a Puerto Rican woman with complications from a botched abortion about once a week.

I told Rosario about the sense of shame and the moral ambivalence some of my respondents expressed and asked if she could account for the difference between these women and the women in her mother's generation in New York. She suggested several possibilities: (1) the women of her mother's generation were very poor, and striving to "make it" in the U.S; (2) no contraception of any kind was available;(3) these women had no power to refuse sex; and 4) abortion was preferable to an "*angelita*," or infant mortality, due not to overt neglect, but to the mother being simply overwhelmed.

Some written accounts of illegal abortion also suggest that abortion was not the moral dilemma that it is today. The conservative trend in recent Supreme Court decisions about abortion has motivated many women to come forward with their own abortion narratives (e.g. Bonavolglia 1991; Messer and May 1988; Townsend and Perkins 1992; and Miller 1993) in order to enhance support for keeping abortion legal and accessible. These accounts serve, in Richardson's (1990) terms, as a collective story of women's experiences, in opposition to the traditional patriarchal cultural story that abortion is wrong. One of the most comprehensive of these collections in Patricia Miller's (1993) book, *The Worst of Times: Illegal Abortion: Survivors, Practitioners, Coroners, Cops, and Children of Women Who Died Talk About its Horrors*. It is especially valuable because almost all of these stories are centered in one locality, Pittsburgh, Pennsylvania, and, in several instances, Miller provides several accounts of the same person or event. She talks about some of the similarities in the women's stories. Like Caroline, Carmen, and Rosario's family members, these women did not experience their abortion as a moral problem:

> The similarities among the women who speak here are more striking than the differences, especially considering their diversity in age, race, religion, and class. A number of them had been taught that abortion was morally wrong, but that appears not to have mattered when they were confronted with what they considered impossible pregnancies. Indeed, for most of them, there wasn't even a conflict, a moral dilemma to wrestled with. Their lack of ambivalence is striking (5).

The public controversy about abortion that has erupted around the *Roe v. Wade* Supreme Court decision legalizing abortion has undoubtedly contributed to the moral dilemma some women experience when they consider abortion. This controversy is fueled by the fact that abortion was legalized during a period of feminist activism and expanded opportunities for women. The availability of contraception and abortion is essential to women's full participation in education and employment. Abortion, then, has become a magnet for societal and personal ambivalence about female self-determination (Luker 1984; Gordon 1986).

In their account of religious violence and abortion in Pensacola, Florida, Dallas Blanchard and Terry Prewitt (1993) state that:

> Pensacola fundamentalists were not concerned about abortion until the 1973 Supreme Court decision ... [and] ... we can safely predict that abortion would disappear as an issue as long as it was illegal. Indeed, this has been the case in the past. According to a knowledgeable informant, the Enzor Brothers Hospital, about forty miles northeast of Pensacola in Crestview, performed abortions virtually on demand in the 1930's and 1940's ... but there was no public outcry. Thus the fundamentalists' major concern, as shown by their public actions, is public morality — or legalized and positively sanctioned immorality as they define it. As long as the law does not legitimate what they see as immorality, the issue fades from primary attention and concern (233).

In other words, the social fact of legal abortion openly challenges the cultural story that defines non-marital sex as a transgression that must be paid for, and that defines females primarily as mothers (Luker 1984; Gordon 1986).

Another similarity in Miller's (1993) accounts of women's experiences with illegal abortion, and one that is shared with my respondents, is isolation:

> Perhaps the most striking similarity of all is the nearly universal sense of isolation these women describe as they had their underground abortions in frightening and inappropriate places, at the hands of strangers with unknown qualifications. Every woman was alone and terrified, but determined to do whatever was necessary to terminate her pregnancy.
> If so many women were having illegal abortions, how could that sense of isolation have been so pervasive? It is the price of silence, of things hidden. This was abortion underground (6).

Much of this chapter is about what Laurel Richardson terms the cultural story of Puerto Rican women. This is the traditional patriarchal story of virginity, sexual shame, motherhood, and submission to men and male authority. For some Puerto Rican women, especially poor ones, the norm of virginity may have been replaced by one of bounded sexuality (Horowitz 1983), yet this functions in their lives as a minor modification of the cultural story.

Richardson defines the collective story as one which can create a shared consciousness, a feeling of not being alone, or a belief in shared struggle against barriers intrinsic to the social order. Individual acts of resistance, such as aborting a pregnancy, have the potential to become part of a collective story of female self-determination only if they are shared. Richardson states that one response to a collective story is "that's my story. I am not alone" (129). She goes on to explain the "transformative possibilities" of a collective story:

> At the individual level, people make sense of their lives through the stories that are available to them, and they attempt to fit their lives into the available stories. People live by stories. If the available narrative is limiting, destructive, or at odds with the actual life, peoples's lives end up being limited and textually disenfranchised. Collective stories which deviate from standard cultural plots provide new narratives; hearing them legitimates a replotting of one's own life. New narratives offer the patterns for new lives (129).

A key question, then, is how a possibly resistant act, such as getting an abortion or leaving a relationship, becomes redefined from an isolated act to part of a collective story. To answer this question, in chapter five I will discuss the specific cultural values that are part of the individual narratives, how these values worked in each woman's life (e.g. through religion or family) and how these values affected the abortion experience. In chapter six I will show that, for some women, their experience is a "moral passage" (Addelson 1991) that encourages the beginning of a collective story.

5

The Cultural Story and the Decision to Get an Abortion

In this chapter I will return to the narratives about abortion in order to examine how the cultural story each woman grew up with affected her abortion experience, and how that experience, in turn, might have affected her beliefs. In the course of telling me her story, each woman described certain cultural values (the cultural story) that she grew up with, and may still hold. In some cases, these values were transmitted chiefly by her mother and other family members. In other cases, the woman mentioned her church or her friends, in addition to family, as sources of cultural values. In most cases (fifteen), these values, and the source of these values, had an effect on who the woman told about her pregnancy, or whether she discussed it at all. Ten women stated that the conflict between their upbringing and their decision to get an abortion made the decision difficult. Five stated that they wished they had more time or opportunity to talk about their decision before actually making it. The importance of the family as a source of values, and a needed (but usually unavailable) source of support in the abortion experience indicate the interdependence and respect that characterize Latina family life.

Throughout the narratives, there was little variation about the cultural story. Women's descriptions of their upbringing, whether or not the family was religious, resonate with themes discussed in the previous chapter: virginity prior to marriage, sexual shame, the importance of family, and the belief that abortion is wrong. Only one woman, Mayra, told me that she was raised (by her maternal grandmother) to "make my own choices" about important life decisions. For thirteen women, the abortion experience was in some way empowering. That is, it allowed them to confirm, or reconfirm, that, in Mayra's words, "my life belonged to me."

The Cultural Story About Virginity and Family Life

The women's cultural story is a traditional patriarchal one, centered around virginity. Related themes include sexual shame, getting married to legitimate a pregnancy, and marrying one's first sex partner. Eight women discussed virginity and related themes at length, and a ninth (Mayra) mentioned that she was a virgin when she married.

Marisol, a single mother, had her abortion so that her two daughters could continue their education and she could maintain her employment, and as a way of coping with male abandonment (chapter two). She explained that she had become pregnant with her oldest daughter, now fifteen, when she was fifteen herself. Her then seventeen year old boyfriend was willing to marry her, and they did get married:

> He was seventeen, but he was willing to finish school, live a life together, and raise the child, and we did. ... We were married for eleven years.

Apparently Marisol's family considered the circumstances of her marriage a disgrace, and her mother continues to feel that way:

> My mother to this day -- my daughter turned fifteen yesterday -- doesn't let me forget what I did fifteen years ago. I left home when I was fifteen, to have my baby. So of course, on my daughter's birthday, she had to remind the family. So I had the abortion two weeks ago, and fifteen years ago, I had [my baby].

This juxtaposition of Marisol's abortion, her first pregnancy at age fifteen, and her daughter's fifteenth birthday party was very hurtful to her.

Virginity as a defining characteristic of a good woman or a good wife was an important part of Felice's and Miriam's stories. Felice's pregnancy and abortion (chapter two) resulted from her first sexual encounter at age seventeen. Had she continued her pregnancy (and revealed her sexual behavior), she believes that she would have been "kicked out of the house." Her experience "scared me from the guys." Three years later, she married "the same guy," in part because she was afraid that no one else would want to marry her: "Who would want me if I'm not a virgin?"

Miriam described her mother's non-marital relationship to her father, and how difficult her mother's life was as a result. She suggested that, if she had revealed her unplanned pregnancy to anyone, it would have confirmed both her own and her mother's worthlessness:

I come from a family that, my mother never married my father. My father was a married man when my mother had me and my brother. They had gone out before. Her family didn't like him, and sent her to New York. Mother returned, and 'they eloped,' [and she had me and my brother, and then they broke up]. My mother lived a life as a marginal woman. In Puerto Rico if you do not marry your husband, you're worthless, you're nothing. Your worth is defined by having a male next to you, and my mother never married. And she lived all her life, as an exemplary life, to prove to the community that she was a good woman, and she was a good woman. ... It occurred to me, about a month ago, that one of the reasons why I did it [had the abortion] was because for me to have that child would have meant that she failed. I would be her failure. She was a single mother, and like mother, like father, like son, like mother, like daughter, and if I had had that baby, I would have been the proof that the rest of the community wanted, that she was no good, that she had worked this hard for nothing, because her daughter, just like she did, got pregnant and now has this child. She went off to school, but the school didn't do any good. I would have been her failure.

Like the stories of Felice and Marisol, Miriam's story illustrates the humiliation and disgrace of non-marital pregnancy and birth.

Several women went beyond the idea of marrying to legitimate a pregnancy and explained that the norm in their family was for the woman to marry her first sex partner. Carmen described how her mother tried to force her to do this:

I had had only one previous sexual relationship. [I had] gone out with this guy, it was like date rape, but that [the concept of date rape] didn't exist then. My mother put me an Audy Home. I'd gone out with this guy, and he raped me. My sister knew what happened. I was in there [the Audy Home] about a month. [Your mother put you in the Audy Home?] She thought I had run away with him. He put me in an apartment [and kept me there]. I ran out and told my sister. His mother begged me not to make a complaint. My mother said I should be with him since he had taken away my virginity. In Puerto Rico, if a man does that, you have to be with him. I didn't want to be with him. She said 'stay with him or I will put you away.' So she put me. Remember, when I was in school, that's how it used to be. If your parents say you are bad, if they say you ran away [they can put you in a juvenile home].

Carmen's stay at the Audy Home was followed by her second, violent relationship (chapter three) and an illegal abortion (chapter two). Having survived all this and raised four daughters, Carmen now describes herself as "relaxed, more sure of myself." She is employed at a job she likes, working as a health advocate.

The cultural story about family life includes both pro-natalism and male dominance. Women's experiences with men and their beliefs about gender relationships are the subject of chapters three and four. Pronatalism was generally brought up in connection with the idea that abortion is wrong. Several women mentioned the importance of marriage as central to female identity. One who emphasized the importance of marriage is Diana. Diana grew up with mixed messages about abortion. She said her mother is so religious, "she could be the pope." Nevertheless, Diana was aware that her mother had more than one abortion. In fact, Diana's sixteenth birthday party was canceled because her mother needed the money she would have spent on the party to pay for her (the mother's) abortion. Diana has not told her mother about any of her abortions because she believes that her mother would not understand or approve of them. The difference lies in the fact that Diana's mother was married and had several children and she had her abortions, presumably, for the well-being of the entire family. Diana, in contrast, was thirty-one at the time of our interview, a student, and single. Her mother wishes she would get married, settle down, and have a family.

The Cultural Story About Abortion

Eighteen women said that they were brought up to believe that abortion is "wrong," "a sin," or that women who have abortions "burn in hell." The exceptions (Diana and Mayra) were discussed earlier in this chapter. Ten women said that, at the time they decided to get an abortion, they were aware that they were going against their families' beliefs, or their culture, rather than their own religious beliefs. Six women who were practicing Catholics at the time of the abortion did not indicate that getting an abortion created a crisis of faith for them. Rather, they felt a generalized lack of support from a Catholic-based culture. That is, Catholicism (or Protestantism) had an indirect effect on the abortion experience, through the family and the generalized culture.

Alicia's story is an illustration of the indirect effect of Catholicism on her abortion experience. Alicia was one of ten children, born in Puerto Rico, and raised Catholic. When she was seventeen, her parents moved to Chicago with their two youngest children, Alicia and her sister. Eventually Alicia went to college and got married. She and her husband were both students, active in Puerto Rican student politics, and not religious, when Alicia got pregnant. Getting the abortion was her husband's idea. Although Alicia agreed with him about the abortion, she thinks she did not have enough time to think about what she wanted to do. She believed that some of her student friends would have supported her decision, but her family would not. She explained that:

> I was very ashamed of what I was going to do. [Do you remember why?] I guess because [even though my closest friends probably would have supported me], I guess my upbringing -- I was brought up as a Catholic, my family's very religious -- I felt I was doing wrong.

She went on to say that

> At the university there were progressive students, and I thought it should be a woman's choice, but my upbringing conflicted with my new ideology. ... When I had it, I was becoming more aware of women's rights, and I definitely think that only the woman can make that choice, but I still had doubts.

Alicia summed up her narrative this way:

> [There are] things about my upbringing I don't care for, like religion, but the fact that I was very poor, and had to struggle all my life, and the fact that my parents were a good example, and that my brothers and sisters all wanted an education, the fact that I had that upbringing and I was able to follow it -- I saw so many people drop out of programs, with many kids, and low income, I feel I have 'made it.' As much as I like to think I am over my upbringing, if I'm very honest with you, I still would not mention the fact that I've had two abortions with some of my close friends, because I guess it is sort of a shameful thing, even though I do feel comfortable with it.

Alicia told me that she has participated in clinic defense (helping patients enter an abortion clinic when anti-abortion protesters are present) and that she would speak at a pro-choice rally.

Another narrative that illustrates the indirect power of Catholicism through the family and generalized culture is Ana's. Chapter two relates Ana's story of her abortion, obtained at a time when she had three children and her partner was a violent problem drinker. She has regretted the abortion ever since, and still holds it against her partner, even though he has stopped drinking and helps with the care of their four children. When I asked Ana about her upbringing she told me she is not religious, although she has occasionally attended a Disciples of Christ church when invited. Ana's mother is Catholic and her father "used to be Catholic" but when Ana was a child, her family hardly ever went to mass. Nevertheless, Ana said that whenever anyone in her family of origin heard about an abortion, "they would start talking real bad about that person." Whenever abortion as a topic came up, the reaction was " 'oh my God, the people that do that [get abortions].'" Ana told me she would like to be able to talk to her mother about her abortion but she just can't. She described one visit with her mother, in Puerto Rico, when her youngest was a baby:

> once, I was about to tell my mother, when I had my baby. I was unhappy and my mother asked 'why? you have a beautiful baby.' He was so beautiful and I felt so guilty [about aborting my previous pregnancy]. I was about to tell her, but I just said I was tired. I'm ashamed also.

Ana's eleven year old daughter has also talked against "people who kill the baby inside the stomach." After her daughter said this, explained Ana, "I couldn't say nothing." She added, "I'll never tell my daughter that [about the abortion], even when she's big." For much of her life Ana has moved back and forth between the mainland and the island (Puerto Rico). When I interviewed her she was living in transitional housing. When I asked about her friends, she replied that she has few friends.

Lucy is the only practicing Catholic who shared the abortion decision with her mother, who is also a practicing Catholic. Lucy explained how her mother helped her decide what to do about her pregnancy using a cultural norm that is not Catholic. Lucy explained that

> we [Puerto Ricans] have a saying that 'when you have one child, you can fit anywhere. When you have two or three, it bothers people. They will keep you for a week or two, then throw you out.

Her mother also advised her to "think about what you want."

I was not familiar with the belief about a single woman "fitting in" better with one child. After this interview, as part of my search for women to interview, I gave a presentation about reproductive issues and a description of my research to a class of Latinas studying in preparation for the G.E.D. examination. As I related Lucy's story, women smiled or nodded their heads in recognition of something familiar to them. However, no other woman I interviewed related similar advice from anyone she shared her abortion decision with.

Four women described their abortion experience as a direct challenge to their own faith. Marisol (chapter two) explained that before her abortion she "used to think of myself as a good person," and believed that "a child is a blessing, [but with the abortion], I took that away from myself." She continued:

> I hope God can forgive me, and I can forgive myself.

[Do you think God can?]
No.

At this point, Marisol began to cry. When we resumed the conversation, I gave Marisol the name of a counselor as well as my own phone number in case she wanted to talk some more.

Describing the day of her abortion, Marisol explained that

> the worst part was laying on the table, asking God to forgive me, asking the baby to forgive me. [I was] feeling ugly, [and felt] hatred, not for him [her partner], but for myself, that's when I really started disliking myself.

Toward the end of the interview I asked Marisol if she thought she had made the right decision about her pregnancy. She replied,

> no [long pause], not the right decision, but it was maybe the best decision at that time, but the right decision? It was best in terms of the situation, yes, but as right or wrong ..."

Marisol has experienced how difficult, and how important, making a decision about how to resolve a problem pregnancy is. She described how she would advise a friend in such a situation:

> [I would tell her] to make sure it's exactly what she wants, whatever decision she is making is what she really wants, not because its the right thing or the wrong thing or the best thing. This is what she, personally, wants to do -- have the baby, have an abortion, give the baby up. She's the one that's got to live with it.

Religion is very important to Marisol, and she is resentful that her church is unwilling to support her when she needs support:

> I want help and they can't give it. ... That's why -- the Catholic religion -- I'm angry at them. The way they have brought me up, it's not a place I can go to for comfort [and] I need for God to forgive me.

The Haunting Effects of the Cultural Story
on the Abortion Experience

During each interview, I asked each woman to describe the day she got the abortion, including who, if anyone, accompanied her and what she thought about when the abortion was over. Most women mentioned being hungry, feelings of relief, or just wanting to go home. Two women who said they did not practice a religion at the time of their pregnancy and abortion or at the time of our interview told me about threatening religious images they experienced as they lay in the recovery room.

Gloria's abortion narrative, involving her husband's immature and emotionally abusive behavior, is related in chapter two. As she described the day of her abortion, she said that she felt "trapped" and "evil" as the abortion proceeded. When the abortion was over she felt "waves of heat" and saw "an image -- like a Devil." She emphasized that she was, and is, a nominal, non-practicing Catholic. Nevertheless, the image of the Devil was "a spiritual thing to me." She explained that, "because I was working and going to school and accepted these for myself, I anticipated feeling okay about the abortion." Reflecting on her upbringing, she concluded that, "the feeling I had was not surprising [considering my upbringing] to put children ahead of my own career and well-being."

The intensity of Gloria's experience with the evil image led her to believe for a while after the abortion that she had done the wrong thing, and "traded one bad situation for another." Her husband's subsequent behavior has convinced her that their marriage is definitely over, and she says that her life is "much better than before: I've come out of a living hell [her relationship to an emotionally abusive husband]." Returning to her feelings about her abortion Gloria said that, "only recently, in the last year, have I come to the acceptance that me and my husband aren't going to work it out [and that I made the right decision]."

Diana described her upbringing in Jersey City as "heavy duty Spanish Catholic, but I rebelled every inch of the way." She added that she is not "a Bible-thumper like my mother." She remarked later that "my mother could be the Pope" and speculated that if her husband (Diana's father) died, she might return to Puerto Rico and become a nun. Diana described herself, as a girl, as not afraid of God, but afraid of her mother, with respect to boys, sex, and the like. In spite of her religion, Diana's mother had more than one abortion. Recall that she had to cancel Diana's sixteenth birthday party because she needed the party money for an abortion.

The focus of my interview with Diana, at her request, was her fourth and most recent abortion, which had taken place within the previous six months. She described her experience in the recovery room:

> Looking out the window, I saw a chimney. Just at the time I was looking at it, this huge void swept over me, a rush of emptiness, like someone ripped in my heart, took my being from me. It was horrible. I've had feelings like that before. I remember when I was sixteen and feeling depressed. I don't know if it was so much from the abortion. It was the feeling that I didn't know myself yet.

Diana explained that before the abortion she was feeling "guilty" about her three previous abortions, and thinking that she "should be planning a family" now that she is over thirty and is in a serious relationship. She was thinking that

> God will punish me, maybe by making me sterile, or causing harm to a child I bear. When I think of God in that way, it's a male God. I think of a man's hand coming out of the sky.

Later in the interview we returned to the matter of religious upbringing. Diana reiterated the "maleness" of God as a punishing God, and the residual effect of a Catholic upbringing on her present day feelings:

> It's true what they say about the Catholic Church. If they get you for the first seven years of your life, they have the rest of your life. It's sort of true. The way I think about guilt and punishment, it's still this heaven and hell. When I thought about being punished [for my abortions by being unable to have children] it's always this *male*, something from the sky.

Diana believes that her abortion experience changed her by confirming for her that "I'm the only one who can take care of myself." Diana is an art student, and describes her situation as "just starting to come in to something" both academically and personally. She described each of her previous abortions as "a given" because at the time of each of these pregnancies, the relationship was over or almost over.

Toward the end of each interview, I asked each woman if she thought she had made the right decision about her pregnancy. Sixteen women answered with an unequivocal yes. The responses of Gloria (only recently has she come to accept her decision) and Marisol (not a right decision but the best one) are discussed above. Ana's account, which ends with her belief that abortion should be illegal, is presented in chapter two, as is Cherrie's, in which she regrets both abortions, does not judge other women who get abortions, and has reconciled this with the strict teachings of the Baptist church.

Nevertheless, acceptance of one's decision to get an abortion has different meanings. For some women caught in a "spiral of silence" (Noelle-Neuman 1974) their abortion remains a shameful secret. Other women experienced the abortion, and perhaps other events surrounding the abortion, as empowering. For these women, the abortion served as a "moral passage" (Addelson 1991) to a new definition of self and the beginning of a collective story.

6

Abortion as a Moral Passage to a Collective Story

As each woman described her abortion experience, she integrated it into her life at the time she was pregnant, and into her life as a whole. Chapter two focuses on the abortion experience itself and what it meant to individual women. In this chapter I will examine more closely how individual women, looking back on their abortion experience, integrate it into their life as a whole. For some women, the abortion remains a shameful secret. For others, it is part of a process of empowerment. Some narratives do not fall into either group, but share characteristics of each.

Kathryn Pyne Addelson's notion of "moral passages" provides a useful way to think about how experiences are integrated into one's life. Addelson describes herself as "an analytic philosopher [who] started becoming a sociologist in 1974 when I attended Howard Becker's class in field methods" (1991 [1988]:129, f.1). She discusses the usefulness of Becker's symbolic interactionist methodology to her work as a philosopher in two essays that examine abortion as a moral issue. The first, "Moral Revolution" (1991 [1977]) uses an interview with a member of Jane, an illegal abortion collective that operated in Chicago between 1969 and 1973 to contrast two ways of thinking about abortion. The first is the familiar idea of abortion as a conflict between the rights of the fetus and the rights of the woman. A second, more fruitful approach is the redefinition of abortion as enacted by the Jane collective. Addelson explains that, for members of the Jane collective, the underlying goal was one of "meaningful lives for women, or a free choice among alternatives for meaningful lives" (54). The members of Jane redefined abortion from an abstract, contested right to a resource a woman might need in order to live a meaningful life.

Addelson continues her analysis of how morality emerges out of people's interactions in her essay, "Moral Passages" (1991 [1985]). Here she examines several "passages" from girlhood to womanhood, including pregnancy/abortion and pregnancy/unwed motherhood. In using "unwed motherhood" as an example of a moral passage, Addelson presents her analysis of a study by Prudence Rains, *Becoming an Unwed Mother* (1971), in which Rain compares pregnant young women at two maternity homes for white middle class girls and a day school for pregnant black girls. The social workers at one maternity home organize the experiences of the girls in their care in such a way that these girls realign themselves with the conventional morality of marriage and motherhood. They do this by conceptualizing the young pregnant girl as a "good girl" who "made a mistake," or "was led astray" but who "learned from her mistake" and, after giving birth and surrendering the child for adoption, remains a "good girl," that is, someone who will make a good wife someday. Conventional thinking, the cultural story of marriage and motherhood, remains firmly in place here.

At the project school, the young black residents are more skeptical of the social workers and resent their attempts to pry into their personal lives. They, too, believe they have "made a mistake" but, in general, intend to raise their children and remain in school. Marriage was often seen as an obstacle to remaining in school. Not getting married, and remaining in school, then, was a respectable strategy for being a good mother within this community.

Rains did her research in the late sixties, when abortion was illegal and social and cultural support for single mothers, and unmarried women generally, barely existed. Although a young black teen who raised her baby was accepted within her family and neighborhood, the general perception of these girls within the mainstream U.S. culture was that they were immoral and a burden to taxpayers (Solinger 1992). Addelson's account of Rains' work highlights the importance of social context as well as personal resources. Since Rains did her research, abortion has become legal and available and, as one result of feminism and other social movements, there is some social and cultural support for single mothers. The stigma attached to young low income mothers who receive welfare, however, remains.

Addelson explains that morality emerges out of people's interactions, and emphasizes the importance of placing these experiences within the context of women's lives, and within the context of social support, or lack of support, for meaningful lives. As women make such passages, they can either realign themselves with conventional thinking (the cultural story) or create a new definition of themselves and their behavior.

Given the range of outcomes possible in this idea of a moral passage, and given the intensity of the abortion experience as related by each of my respondents, it is reasonable to think about each narrative as a description of a moral passage. Yet the question remains -- a passage to what? One possible outcome of a moral passage is, in Addelson's terms, a realignment with conventional thinking, or, in Laurel Richardson's terms, a reaffirmation of the cultural story. Another possible out-come is a rejection or redefinition of received ideas and the potential for a collective story. The creation of a collective story is not a given. In order for one to exist, individual women must share their ideas with each other. A moral passage to the possibility of a collective story oc-curs when women redefine a common experience that has moral over-tones within the cultural story, and share their experiences, and their insights, with each other.

Redefining the Meaning of Abortion and Womanhood

Central to the collective story of these narratives is self-determination and resisting male control. For most of these women, getting an abor-tion meant that they were able to maintain opportunities for themselves by remaining in school or leaving confining relationships. What the abortion meant to each woman at the time she obtained it was almost perfectly correlated with whether or not she has redefined abortion from a "wrong" or a "sin" to a more positive definition of abortion as something a woman might need in order to live a meaningful life. Women who obtained abortions as a way of "keeping on being who they were" or as a way of resisting male control have redefined abortion in this way, while those for whom the abortion was a way of coping with male abandonment have retained a definition of abortion as wrong. Every woman but Ana is pro-choice, in that each one believes that decision-making belongs to the pregnant woman, but the second group maintains a definition of abortion as wrong, or a sin that God will forgive.

Another variable correlated almost as closely as the meaning of abortion for the woman's life is whether or not the respondent had any support for her decision. Those women who knew someone who had gotten an abortion, or received support for their own decision, were more likely than the others to redefine abortion positively.

Shameful Secrets and the Spiral of Silence

Five women, Ana, Gloria, Cherrie, Marisol and Mercedes, maintain a definition of abortion as wrong. Ana is anti-choice and thinks that abortion should be illegal. The story of her abortion is told in chapter two. Her narrative makes clear the interaction between abortion as a strategy for dealing with male abandonment, total lack of support for abortion as an acceptable act, and lack of material resources, resulting in a definition of abortion as a shameful secret, and her interview with me as part of her recovery. Recall that when Ana discovered her preg-nancy, she had three young children by her partner, who at this time had a drinking problem and was violent toward her. He was not happy about Ana's pregnancy and offered to "look for the money" to pay for an abortion. Ana blames the abortion on her partner and on the clinic (simply for being there). She has a fourth child by this partner, he has quit drinking and he now helps care for the children, yet she cannot forgive him for the abortion. According to her narrative, Ana knows no one, either prior to or since the abortion, who has indicated a positive or neutral opinion about abortion. Her entire family of origin, and her own daughter, are outspoken in their condemnation of it. Additionally, at the time of our interview, Ana did not have a permanent home, but was living in temporary housing provided by a social service agency and working "off the books" at a sub-minimum wage. She framed our interview as "my chance to talk" because "I had never talked to nobody [about the abortion]."

Ana's story provides an example of someone who is trapped in a "spiral of silence" (Noelle-Nuemann 1974). In her discussion of the formation of public opinion about controversial issues, Elisabeth Noelle-Neumann argues that "public opinion arises from an interaction of individuals with their social environment" in that each person "[observes her] social environment, by assessing the distribution of opinions for and against [her] ideas, but above all by evaluating the strength (commitments), the urgency, and the chances of success of certain proposals and viewpoints" (1974:43-44). In Ana's case, virtually all of the opinions about abortion that she was and is aware of in her immediate environment are negative. Additionally, they are vehemently expressed (e.g."Oh my God, the people that do that"). In such an environment, the fear of moral isolation is a reasonable one. Noelle-Neuman explains that, for many people, not isolating oneself from those one is close to is even more important than validating one's own judgement. Ana told me she would like to be able to talk to her mother about her abortion, but she is afraid to. Her interview with me was her "chance to talk," probably her only one. Although I suggested that she call Planned Parenthood for counseling, I doubt, given her noncommittal response and her lack of resources, that she will do so.

Cherrie's two abortions were in response to male abandonment and an uncertain relationship. She regrets both of them. Like Ana, she has no support from anyone close to her for the idea that getting an abortion is an acceptable act. Additionally, Cherrie attends a Baptist church well known for its anti-abortion stance. Nevertheless she supports the availability of abortion. Recall her account in chapter two in which she explained that everybody has to do whatever they think. It's not good to have an abortion, but the way that we live, with teenagers and so many problems, they're going to find somebody to do it.

She added that,"little by little, I understand that He forgives me, that I have to live. I can't deal with that by myself. I leave that to God.

Unlike Ana, Cherrie is deeply religious, and has someone (God) to talk to. Also unlike Ana, Cherrie has a powerful reason to believe that it should be possible to obtain an abortion under standard medical conditions: her own mother died of an illegal abortion at the age of twenty-six.

I obtained interviews with Cherrie and Ana in response to the personal ad in the *Extra*. Both of them welcomed a chance to talk about a painful experience. Cherrie explained that she saw my ad as

> part of my own recuperation, because its nothing you talk about to nobody, but because I don't know you and you are not part of my family, and its something that maybe can help you or others, I do it, but not because it's easy.

Ana and Cherrie are the only two women who regret their abortions. They are also the only two who explicitly stated that the interview was part of their recuperation from a painful experience.

An example of someone whose abortion experience contains elements of both empowerment and shame is provided by Julia. Recall that Julia obtained an abortion at the age of fifteen, and that she already had a daughter by this partner. Prior to her abortion, she did not share her plans with anyone, because she sensed that her friends, her partner, and her grandmother (who raised her) would disapprove or try to stop her. Julia located an abortion clinic in the Yellow Pages and went there by herself. Subsequently, her partner discovered what she had done, and they "got into a fight and we left each other."

Looking back on her abortion, Julia has conflicting feelings about it. She is proud of herself that, as a fifteen year old, she obtained an abortion completely on her own: "I outsmarted them. I outsmarted everybody. I outsmarted my mother (grandmother). I outsmarted the father of the child. ... I knew what I was doing." Julia also describes herself as "a spoiled brat" who was indulged by her grandparents. She added that

> God's going to punish me for what I did. [Why?] It says in the Bible, because I have been to church a couple of times lately — not saying I'm religious or nothing — but I have been to church and I have heard people say that it's wrong, that God gave him life in my stomach.

In response to a question about her religion, Julia replied:

> [If I were filling out a form] I would say 'none'. I would say 'Catholic'
> but I would say 'none' to be honest. [Why would you say 'Catholic'?]
> Because I was baptized Catholic, that's why I would say 'Catholic'.
> Every time when I have the babies [she has six children], they say
> 'what's your religion?' I say 'Catholic.'

The lesson Julia would like to convey to her daughter Helen about her
(Julia's) girlhood is

> I don't want her to make the same mistake I did. [My] mistake was that I
> opened my legs before time. I didn't enjoy my young life like other girls
> did. I want her to enjoy life, and wait.

Helen's father (the partner in the aborted pregnancy) provides financial
support for her and Helen spends every other weekend with him. As
Julia describes their relationship now: "I see him as the father of my
daughter. I choose him as my best friend. We should never have had
no affair." Both of these statements indicate Julia's belief that having
sex at a young age is a mistake, and she does not mention the use of
birth control. Nevertheless, while describing her partner's violent reaction to discovering the abortion, Julia said, "it was my decision, it was
my stomach, it was my body. Who was he to tell me what to do?"

Throughout the interview I asked Julia about her contradictory feelings about abortion, and she acknowledged, but couldn't really explain
them. Julia's abortion is one of the most "public" in my sample in that
her whole family seems to know about it. Yet the idea of helping someone make a decision about a pregnancy is incomprehensible to her. After all, she says, no one helped her, and she was only fifteen.

Redefining Abortion as an Acceptable Act

The idea that women are entitled to make choices that enable them to
live meaningful, self-determined lives stands in opposition to the patriarchal cultural story. Fourteen women frame abortion this way -- as a
procedure that enabled them to live a meaningful life as they defined it.
For many of them, the abortion experience itself formed a moral passage
to this belief about themselves. For others, the abortion coupled with
ending a relationship formed this passage. Women whose abortion allowed them to keep on being who they were or resist male control generally have positive beliefs about abortion, as do those who had some
support for their decision.

Felice's narrative provides an example of a young woman whose
abortion was initially a source of shame, but eventually became part of a

moral passage to self-affirmation and a career that she is proud of. When Felice discovered her pregnancy she was about to graduate from high school and had "lots of plans -- I had just won a scholarship to Northeastern, which at that time was a big deal, for a Puerto Rican girl to get a scholarship." Felice was ashamed of her pregnancy. She said that she knew nothing about sex or pregnancy and had no one to talk to about these things. She was not in a relationship with the partner, although he did not want Felice to abort the pregnancy because it was "his baby" and "he was very Catholic -- it's a sin." He offered to marry Felice, but they had "no money, no place, and besides, I wanted to go to college." Ironically, when Felice noticed symptoms of her pregnancy, it was her partner who suggested seeing a doctor, and the doctor presented Felice with the choice of aborting or continuing the pregnancy.

Felice described her mother as "the queen of the house" and very much opposed to sex outside of marriage and to abortion. Felice characterized herself as her mother's "pride and joy -- I was the only one in the family with any brains." She thought that if she had continued her pregnancy, she would have let her mother down, would have been "kicked out of the house [and] would lose my scholarship."

Felice's prior opinion about abortion is that she "knew it was there," especially as "a way when you have too many kids." Her sister-in-law had had one, and a high school friend of Felice's had told Felice about hers. Despite this modest support, the stress of keeping the pregnancy and abortion a secret from her mother took its toll on Felice: "something snapped," her grades went down, and she did not attend Northeastern until several years later (she kept her scholarship). Looking back, she realized all the stress she was under. "I blew it," she said, "because I had no one to talk to."

Eventually Felice and her partner did get married. She continued working so he could finish school and generally put his plans ahead of her own. They had one child. A few years later, Felice's husband died and she has raised the child alone. When I interviewed Felice, she had earned a degree in social work and worked in a social service agency providing services to teen mothers. She was very articulate about what she thinks these young women need: resources to stay in school, job training, and realistic information about careers and about birth control.

Felice's life experiences have changed her beliefs about herself as a Puerto Rican woman. In response to questions about the relative importance of the husband's and the wife's jobs, and the effect of women's employment on their children (chapter three) she replied that when married, she put her husband's career first, but she has since changed her mind, and describes herself as a feminist. Although she knew as a teenager that abortion "was there" her respect for her mother made her abortion a shameful secret. It took several years to come to terms with it. Now, she says, "my life was changed because a doctor told me my choices." Her pride in her work with teenage girls is evident.

Only one woman, Lucy, described a supportive discussion with her mother prior to her abortion. At age seventeen she had one child by a partner to whom she was not married, but "just together" with. Recall Lucy's description (chapter three) of her partner as old fashioned:

> He was [nine years] older. He wanted things his way. It felt like a fa-
> ther-daughter type relationship. He didn't want me to go out. I couldn't
> go out unless I was with him. [He didn't want me to get my G.E.D. be-
> cause] 'you're a woman – you should stay in the house' – an old fash-
> ioned type.

After they separated, a few years later, Lucy "came out pregnant again" and turned to her mother, her two sisters, and a friend for support. Lucy and her mother are practicing Catholics. Nevertheless, Lucy's mother encouraged her to think about her future, and what would be the best alternative for her. Her sisters and friend provided similar support. I told Lucy that many women did not believe their mothers would be supportive and asked what she thought was different about her situation. She replied that younger girls (Lucy was eighteen) and girls who are financially dependent on the parent(s) might be more afraid to reveal a pregnancy. For Lucy, the cultural story was enacted by her peers (her partner and most of her girlfriends) and undermined by her mother's, sisters', and friend's encouragement to think about her-self and her future. Lucy was clearly concerned about a meaningful life for herself, and framed her choice as "deciding either on having another child and living off public aid or going back to school and getting a de-cent job and raising my first son." Lucy said her decision to get an abortion was not difficult, that she "felt confident with it," and that it was "my very important decision." Lucy described most of her friends as "old-fashioned" about gender relationships and thinks her views are different from theirs. In response to the questions about marriage, work, and children, she replied that both parents should be able to work and share the care of their children, and that her experience with pre-school for one of her children was positive.

These examples have been presented at length to show the impor-tance of personal support for how a woman experiences abortion. These women's experiences are similar to those researched by Mary K. Zimmerman (1977). In her interviews with women at an abortion clinic in Minneapolis, she found that the support and approval of others made the abortion less stressful, and that lack of support did not change the decision, but the experience of it. Additionally, the meaning of the abortion influences whether or not she believes that abortion is an acceptable act. Women who have redefined abortion in this way generally think that they should be able to live meaningful lives as they define them.

Like Felice and Lucy, other women (Alicia, Miriam, Rosa, Evelyn, and Diana) wanted to continue their education. Evelyn had two abortions while she was in college. She explained that the process of deciding what to do about her pregnancies forced her to "evaluate my life" and "made me strong."

For some women (e.g. Carmen and Caroline) obtaining an abortion and leaving a confining relationship occurred together. Mayra (chapter three) had ended her relationship and was in a new one. She saw her abortion experience as part of a "growth spurt" that "confirmed that my life belonged to me." Caroline's experience with an illegal abortion and divorce was described in chapter two. She explained the transformative power of her experience this way:

> Did it change my life: Oh yes. Oh yes. I became a woman. ... I knew what I wanted. I became free. I was able to make decisions on my own. It was the start of being able to determine what's right from what's wrong [for me and] how to guide somebody else in a similar situation.

Sharing Experiences and Beginning a Collective Story

A collective story comes into being when individual stories about common experiences are shared. The importance of women's stories as an alternative to male dominant cultural stories is a feature of feminist scholarship in many disciplines, including history (e.g. Lerner 1993; Personal Narratives Group 1989; Gluck and Patai 1991), literature (e.g. Rich 1979; Heilbrun 1979, 1988) and theology (e.g. Christ 1980; Erickson 1993; Say 1990), as well as sociology. In her examination of the theological implications of women's novels, Elizabeth Say (1990) explains that, "it is through our stories that we come to create and understand ourselves" (4). In her collection of essays, *Writing a Woman's Life*, Carolyn Heilbrun (1988) argues that stories are essential to personal development, and that "women have been deprived of the narratives, or texts, plots, or examples, by which they might assume power over -- take control of -- their own lives" (17). She describes the absence of biography and autobiography that affirms women's self-determination:

> Well into the twentieth century, it continued to be impossible for women to admit in their autobiographical narratives the claim of achievement, the admission of ambition, the recognition that accomplishment was neither luck nor the result of the efforts or generosity of others (24).

The absence of stories about female achievement has serious conse-
quences for young women. Without such stories, they may not believe
in their own talents, or believe that they have a right to develop them.
Stories about female self-determination and resistance to male control
provide alternatives to the patriarchal cultural story.

   This research suggested that there is a collective story about Puerto
Rican women who get abortions, and that it stands in contrast to the
traditional cultural story of how Puerto Rican women should live.
Richardson (1990) states that one response to a collective story is "that's
my story. I am not alone" (129). Several women have begun sharing
their stories in the hope of generating just that reaction. Richardson
goes on to explain the "transformative possibilities" of a collective story:

> At the individual level, people make sense of their lives through the sto-
> ries that are available to them, and they attempt to fit their lives into the
> available stories. People live by stories. If the available narrative is
> limiting, destructive, or at odds with the actual life, peoples' lives end up
> being limited and textually disenfranchised. Collective stories which
> deviate from standard cultural plots provide new narratives; hearing
> them legitimates a replotting of one's own life. New narratives offer the
> patterns for new lives (129).

   In order for the collective story of Puerto Rican women who get
abortions to transform the patriarchal cultural story, Puerto Rican
women must develop strategies to make this happen.

   Of course, even the most ardent advocates of legal abortion generally
keep their personal lives to themselves. Additionally, according to virtually all of the women interviewed, Puerto Ricans do not share personal matters with people who are not family members. Nevertheless,
respondents who have a positive definition of abortion have found
ways to share their stories. Some do this through their employment as
teachers, health care workers, and social workers in the Puerto Rican
community. Others create a space to talk within their own families, especially with their daughters (Peterman 1993). This is important. There
was general agreement in both focus groups and interviews that a
daughter does not talk about matters like sex or abortion unless her
mother has previously initiated such a discussion. For a daughter to
take the initiative would indicate a lack of respect. It falls to the mother,
then, to create a space for these conversations to take place.

   Surprisingly, four of the women I interviewed (Caroline, Lupe,
Alicia, and Helena) have gone public, either about their own abortions,
or with a pro-choice point of view. I was not aware of the activities or
the beliefs of any of these women prior to my interviews with them.
Caroline (chapter two) is one of very few Latinas to go public about her

own abortion. She has written and published her autobiography, in Spanish, and one chapter presents her abortion experience. She told me that people often ask why she included that chapter, and her answer is that she is not ashamed of her abortion, and she wants Latinas who have had abortions, or who have considered abortion to know that they are not alone. Caroline's wish that women realize "they are not alone" echoes Laurel Richardson's description of the purpose of a collective story: "that's my story. I am not alone" (1990:129). Helena believes that her abortion must remain a secret from her entire family and her friends, yet she has counseled several young women about their problem pregnancies and she has presented a pro-choice personal view on television, with her face and voice disguised. Recall that Alicia has participated in clinic defense and said that she is willing to speak at a pro-choice rally. Lupe has spoken at pro-choice and feminist events.

Portraying a positive attitude about abortion, or sharing the fact of her own abortion, in the course of her employment is another strategy for building a collective story. Lupe, Felice, and Lydia told me that they do this. I met Lydia in the course of my activity as a clinic escort at the abortion clinic where she works. She provided me with both an informant and a personal interview. She believes that her strict, traditional upbringing allows her to relate to Latina patients with traditional beliefs, and that her abortion experience "made me realize what patients really feel" emotionally and physically.

In her work with teen mothers, Felice presents abortion as an alternative for an unplanned pregnancy. Her spontaneous description of a recent experience is as follows:

> [About three months ago] I took a client and there were protesters outside, and that made her feel like the lowest of the low. She had to have it. It was really horrible the way they were talking and they were screaming and all in the name of God and Christianity. I couldn't understand that at all. She had the most horrible time. [She alternated three times between talking to the protesters and the clinic counselors.] I told her to think about what's going on. The girl was sixteen and the 'father' was not even a boyfriend, but an ex-con who is terrorizing the family and is back in jail, and she already has one baby. Some of the protesters spoke Spanish, and some of them attend the church near her house and recognized her.

This account highlights the importance of personal support and the strength of the cultural story even in the face of abuse.

Lupe is a teacher at an alternative high school with a small, mainly Puerto Rican student body. She is very open with the female students about her own abortions, and she said that some students seek her advice about problem pregnancies. She explained that her students's questions about abortion motivated her to talk about her own. Lupe has spoken at pro-choice rallies, works politically for Puerto Rican independence, and, in answer to a question about her religion, replied "Marxist-Leninist." Nevertheless, Lupe did not share the fact of any of her abortions with her parents, who live in Puerto Rico, for many years. She said that her relationship with her parents has "evolved a lot," and described talking to them about her abortion:

> My mother and my father were really adamant that a women should not have an abortion, and then I told them, 'Well, it's the story of your daughter.' and I told them, 'You shouldn't point your fingers, because you don't know what I've done in my life.' and I kind of shared it with them. They cried. I didn't do it in a way that I wanted to pull them away from me, so we had a long discussion and I explained to them where I stood. So now they respect it, they think women have the right to choose whatever they feel is a good decision. It took us a year and a half to finish our discussion [by letter and telephone], but it was a good discussion.

In general, although these women speak positively about abortion and may share their own experience with patients, students, or clients, and even the general public, they still cannot speak of it with their own family, especially their mothers.

Two accounts that highlight the pain of isolation from family members are those of Lydia and Marisol. Lydia had an abortion at the age of thirty-one. Even though her family knows about her job at the abortion clinic, she believes that her own abortion must remain a secret. The fact that she could not go to her mother for support made her feel "deprived" and "lonely" because "you always want to depend on your family through thick and thin, and I felt like I had this huge secret, that I couldn't talk to anyone but my husband and [one of my] sister[s], no one else in the family." Much later in the interview, when I asked Lydia how she would describe herself, she said

> I like myself. I like myself because I keep looking back at how I was raised, and to have my daughter, who's twenty-two years old, and she has a seven month old baby, my grandson, and to see that she can tell me anything, and I feel she does, that's a great feeling to me, because I still don't have that, and I'm not going to, ever.

Marisol is a single mother of two daughters. When she discovered her pregnancy, she told only her partner, who was unwilling to move in with her, marry her, or be a father to the child. During the interview, I turned off the tape recorder three times because she began to cry. Each time, she wanted to continue, saying that the interview was helpful to her, and that I was the only person she could talk to about her abortion. She said that she had begun to distance herself from her family:

> You do it to yourself. So that way, you don't dislike them, you can still love them. The pain of being outcast by someone you love. If family can't love you, who can? So you outcast yourself. You take yourself away from the family, don't communicate, see them less, so they don't find out. It you stay around the family, one day you will break down, and then you might get the support, but more and more you believe that you won't, so you outcast yourself.

Lydia and Marisol were each about thirty years old when they got their abortions, yet each felt lonely because she couldn't turn to her family, especially her mother, for support. Of the twenty women, only three told their mothers about being pregnant prior to the abortion. Fourteen told their male partners. Two told both their mothers and their partners. Four told absolutely no one.

Seven women are mothers of daughters. Each them women assured me that she has intentionally created a relationship with her daughter(s) whereby these daughters can talk about personal matters without shame. Lydia is proud that her own daughter "can tell me anything" because "I still don't have that, and I'm not going to, ever." Marisol has two daughters, ages fifteen and ten. She remembers having to get married at age fifteen. In fact, her mother publicly reminded her of this at a fifteenth birthday gathering for Marisol's daughter. Marisol contrasts her upbringing with what she is trying to create for her daughters:

> I respect my parents and the family so much, this is something I cannot go to them with. I don't know how. I have a fifteen year old daughter and I'm trying to raise her in the correct way — to have an open mind. To choose to go with this to my own family, its a 'you should have known better' kind of situation. So I had to deal with it on my own and it was very difficult.

When I asked if she thought her fifteen year old daughter could come to her, she said, "yes, we're pretty open with each other." Marisol added that she has told her daughter that it would be better if she postponed sex, and to "make sure you are ready, and if you are going to, please [make sure he] uses a condom."

One of the reasons Carmen has broken her twenty-year silence about her abortion is for the sake of her daughters: "I never want them to have to go through the same thing." When asked if she thought her daughters would feel free to talk with her about contraception and abortion, she replied that they already have. Although Julia's oldest child, a girl, is only eleven, Julia also intends to create an openness to discuss these matters.

It is important to distinguish here between the male-centered cultural story that shapes family life (which many of these respondents reject) and the centrality of the family as source of identity and support. These respondents do not reject their families or the value of family life. Rather, many of them are pained by the wedge the abortion creates between them and their loved ones.

In their article analyzing an essay by Minnie Bruce Pratt, Biddy Martin and Chandra Talpade Mohanty explore the concept of "home." They explain that Pratt, a "white, middle-class, Christian-raised, Southern lesbian" (1986:193), tells how her father characterizes Martin Luther King, Jr., and by implication, all black males, as sexually threatening. What emerges, according to Martin and Mohanty, is "the consideration of the white home in response to a threatening outside" (204). The idea of "home" as a response to a threatening outside also exists with communities of color (Moraga 1986; Friedman 1992), but, of course, the power dynamic between the privileged and the poor is reversed.

Experiences of family, or home, are contradictory. For many of these women their families motivated them to be ambitious and value education, yet discussion of matters such as sexuality were suppressed, and this silence became a barrier to achievement. Martin and Mohanty describe the contradiction this way:

> 'Being home' refers to the place where one lives within familiar, safe, protected boundaries; 'not being home' is a matter of realizing that home was an illusion of coherence and safety based on the exclusion of specific histories of oppression and resistance, the repression of differences even within oneself (196).

The women in this study generally value home and family. Some of them talked about the contradictions inherent in this, and have strategized about how to expand the boundaries of what is acceptable "at home."

In order for the collective story of Puerto Rican women who get abortions to transform the patriarchal cultural story, Puerto Rican women must develop strategies to make this happen that are consistent with Puerto Rican family life, including the norms of interdependence and respect. A defining characteristic of respect in Latina family life is not openly challenging the norms, values, and rules of the family. Young Latinas who disagree with their parents' values or engage in behavior that violates the rules believe that lying and secrecy about this is more respectful than open rebellion or a direct challenge. Given this definition of respect, the women I have interviewed who have daughters have chosen a promising strategy. By bringing up subjects like sex, contraception, and abortion themselves, and by suggesting that they will be "open minded" and supportive (while encouraging responsibility) these women are allowing their daughters to talk about these matters without having to define themselves as disrespectful and without having to hide their behavior. These women are creating a space that allows a collective story to emerge.

7

Conclusion: Puerto Rican Women Creating a Collective Story

Contrary to popular stereotypes about Latinas, this research suggests that many Puerto Rican women do not accept traditional gender roles for themselves. A majority of these women have redefined abortion in a positive way, and their accounts suggest that they value egalitarian relationships rather than male centered ones.

There are two sources for the stereotype that Puerto Rican women accept the cultural story, a religious one and a political one. According to the religiously based variant, Latina culture values *marianismo*, or veneration of the Virgin Mary, and an acceptance of virginity, marriage and motherhood as essential to being a good woman (Burgos and Diaz Perez 1986; Campbell 1984). This characterization is similar to the version of the cultural story most of my these women and the older focus group grew up with. These cultural values are powerful influences in the lives of Puerto Rican women, yet many women are beginning to question or reject them.

A politically radical (yet gender conservative) version argues that when a Latina transgresses a gender boundary, for example, by working for wages or getting an abortion, she does so only because she is poor (Russo 1991). In the case of abortion, this theory suggests that Latina women have abortions mainly for economic reasons, in that they continue to see themselves as mothers (or mothers and wives) who are simply too poor to have another child. The economic resources of each woman clearly affected how she was able to cope with her situation (e.g. Carmen's self-abortion with a toothbrush), and what opportunities were available to her. It is equally clear that many of my respondents reject the cultural story for themselves. Having an abortion allowed these women some control in determining the course of their lives. It allowed them to maintain whatever opportunities they had.

Before proceeding further with the main argument of this chapter, I will examine how poverty has affected Puerto Rican women's lives, and how it may have altered the cultural story. Recall that Puerto Ricans have the highest poverty rate among minorities in general, and among Latino minorities, and this is true for Puerto Ricans in Chicago as well as Puerto Ricans nationwide (Robles 1988). Additionally, members of a minority group who are poor are far more likely than poor whites to live in racially or ethnically segregated neighborhoods (Jargowsky and Bane 1990). There is a vast literature (e.g. Amott 1993; Anderson 1990; Wilson 1987) on the decline of urban economies and the national economy, and the effect of this decline on family and personal life. Briefly, young adults from low income neighborhoods face bleak job opportunities and have fewer resources with which to form a household. They are less likely, then, in marry in order to legitimate a pregnancy. The discussion with the younger focus group indicates how this economic reality has affected them. Remaining a virgin until marriage was not brought up as an issue in this group. None was married and six (of twelve) were mothers. For some women, "bounded sexuality" (Horowitz 1983) may have replaced virginity as a norm of sexual virtue. Bounded sexuality implies having sex out of love for the boyfriend, not using contraception (i.e. not planning to have sex), having the baby, and being a good mother.

Although bounded sexuality may have replaced virginity as a norm of sexual virtue, pronatalist values and the idea that motherhood is the core of female identity remain firmly in place. These young women, however, were critical of male dominance. Much of the discussion was about their boyfriends' behavior, and their boyfriends' attempts to control their (the girls') behavior, and how to resist male control. The acceptance of single motherhood, then, may indicate both an acceptance of motherhood as a source of identity and a rejection of a submissive role in relationships. These gender factors interact with class (poverty and decreasing job opportunities), resulting in increasing numbers of single-mother households.

How women experience pregnancy, motherhood, and abortion is determined by many factors, including the strength of their support systems, their religious beliefs, their desire to have children, their opportunities, and their economic resources. These factors interact to make certain choices more or less likely, and the experience of these choices more or less stressful. Each of the twenty women in some way integrated her decision to get an abortion into the rest of her life. She considered what her life would be like if she did or did not get an abortion. Four themes emerged from these narratives that characterized the meaning of abortion for individual women. They are: "keeping on being who I was," preserving life or health, resisting male control, and coping with male abandonment. One woman had an abortion because continuing the pregnancy might have killed her. I am leaving her out of the following analysis because the basis of her decision was medical and not personal.

For each of twelve women who wanted to "keep on being who I was" getting an abortion allowed her to continue her education or maintain job opportunities. For each of ten women, the outcome of the pregnancy was influenced by her relationship to her partner. Four of these ten obtained an abortion as an act of resistance to male control and six as a way of coping with abandonment. For some women, the abortion had more than one meaning.

The meaning of the abortion appears to have had some effect on the difficulty of the decision. Women for whom the abortion allowed them to keep on being who they were, or to resist male control, were evenly split about how difficult the decision was for them. Eight described it as easy and eight described it as difficult. The six respondents who were coping with abandonment, on the other hand, all described their decisions as difficult. Interestingly, one of the "keeping on being" women, Marisol, whose decision was difficult was also coping with abandonment. Sylvia's abortion was both an act of resisting male control and a way of coping with abandonment, and she also experienced the decision as difficult.

In addition to influencing the decision itself, the meaning of the abortion was almost perfectly correlated with whether or not the woman maintained a definition of abortion as wrong, as the women who were coping with abandonment did, or as something she needed to maintain a meaningful life for herself, as the others did. This second group of women, those whose abortions allowed them to "keep on being who they were" or resist male control, acted in contradiction to the cultural story of legitimating a pregnancy by getting married, defining oneself primarily as a mother, and accepting a male dominant relationship.

In general, women valued relationships with men but rejected the idea of male control. The "ideal relationship" for the women in each of the two focus groups was characterized by "sharing" and "trust." In answer to questions about employment and child rearing, most respondents expressed a preference for a relationship in which both parties shared these responsibilities. Respondents valued the "good" relationships they once had, or were currently in. Lydia, for example, described her marriage: "We're the best thing that can happen to one another." Ten women mentioned violence as part of a relationship. Of these, one remains in such a relationship.

The cultural story of virginity (or bounded sexuality), motherhood, and male dominated relationships remains a presence in the Puerto Rican community. Nevertheless, many women, including a majority of the women I interviewed, have acted in contradiction to it by continuing their education, leaving confining relationships, and valuing personal goals. For them the abortion experience, while stressful, provided them some measure of empowerment. Recall, for example, Mayra's statement that "when I made the decision to have that abortion, it confirmed that my life belonged to me." Other women, primarily those who were abandoned emotionally or physically by the male partner, maintain a definition of abortion as wrong. For them getting the abortion represented the emotional hurt of a broken relationship, and their narratives are stories of recovery. Each woman without exception believes that her abortion was a significant event in her life. As such, it functions as a "moral passage" (Addelson 1991), an event that forced her to think about her life, and to confirm or challenge the cultural story. Although most of these women do not fully accept the cultural story of Puerto Rican womanhood, and a few reject it entirely, most retain a strong Puerto Rican identity. They reject the idea that being part of the Puerto Rican community requires them to put aside their best interests.

When I began this project, I approached women who worked in health and social service agencies within the Puerto Rican community and asked them to help me find women who would allow me to interview them. This approach was generally not successful, although some of the women I approached eventually offered themselves as interviewees. Their observations about themselves, as positioned in the Puerto Rican community of Chicago, are instructive. Alicia, for example, works at a health clinic and directs a program for pregnant women that she helped design. She compares herself, as a relatively successful woman, to other Puerto Rican women she observes:

> I consider myself fortunate as a Puerto Rican woman growing up in Chicago. I think my experience will be different from most of the Puerto Rican women in Chicago. I think that, for whatever reason, I was able to do things for myself, finish school, get a good paying job. Because I do a lot of work in the community I see a lot of poverty. I see a lot of women that either don't work or are underpaid, and are very controlled by their husbands and by their financial situation. Even though I was in the same boat the first time I had the abortion [as a low income student], I think that my second one was not, and I think that I have been exposed to different ideas. For most of the Puerto Rican women I know, they would have a real hard time making a decision like this, especially twice. The Puerto Rican community is still very religious, and very poor.

Felice also works in the Puerto Rican community, at a social service agency. She directs a program for teenage mothers. Her comments suggest the difficulty of forging an identity for Puerto Rican women in the United States:

> It's a shame that my friends will not talk to you [about their abortions]. We all feel we did the right thing, but we will not talk about it in public. [My friends are] afraid their children will find out, or that they will lose credibility in the Puerto Rican community. We are mixed up. The Puerto Rican community is very mixed up. Wer're hanging on to our traditions and values and our festivals. We're living in the twentieth century with all American values. We don't know how to act in the middle yet, but we will [maintain a contemporary Puerto Rican identity in the U.S.].

Both of these comments were made at the very end of the interviews, when I asked each of them if she had anything she wanted to add to her story. They indicate that the issues raised by the conflict between the cultural and the collective stories are important to them and to the Puerto Rican community.

For those women whose abortions allowed them to keep on being who they were or to resist male control, their abortions generally were part of a process of empowerment. Their collective story of self-determination both contradicts and modifies the cultural story. A consistent theme of both the cultural and collective stories is the interdependence and respect that characterize family life. The experiences of women who were unable to share the fact of their abortion with their mothers has motivated them to create a space for their own daughters to talk to them about sex, contraception, and abortion. By bringing up these matters with their daughters, these respondents are giving these daughters permission to talk about subjects that would otherwise be forbidden. These women continue to value familial interdependence, and they continue to honor the idea of respect. Their strategy allows their daughters to talk with them about personal matters without acting disrespectful.

This research is focused on Puerto Rican women in the United States. It indicates that a central issue for some Puerto Rican women is to what extent patriarchal values define Puerto Rican womanhood. It would be useful, then, to know about Puerto Rican women in Puerto Rico, including whether or not a feminist movement exists there, and how Puerto Rican women in Puerto Rico think about and experience abortion. Going into these matters in detail would require another study. The admittedly sketchy information that follows is intended to suggest that a growing number of women do not believe that accepting male-centered values is intrinsic to being Puerto Rican.

In my telephone interview with "Judith," a sociologist at the University of Puerto Rico, I asked her if there is a femininst movement in Puerto Rico. She replied, "Oh sure." She told me that the second wave of Puerto Rican feminism emerged in the late 1960's, and that during the past decade, Puerto Rican feminists were active around domestic violence and sexual harassment. Their strategies include research, publicity, and lobbying the Puerto Rican legislature. According to Judith, the laws against domestic violence recently passed by the Puerto Rican legislature are "among the most advanced anywhere" (see *Connections* 34 [1990]:20-21). Judith went on to explain that there was an indigenous Puerto Rican feminist movement in the late nineteenth century, before the United States took control of Puerto Rico. The goals of these feminists included education for women and suffrage.

This feminist activism exists within a culture that remains traditional. According to Judith, most Puerto Rican women (about 70%) are not employed outside the home. In her experience, Puerto Rican women are reluctant to openly support abortion as an acceptable act, yet many women obtain them. According to a recent study (the Pro Mujer Study, Azize and Aviles 1993), "the first scientific estimate of the number of abortions performed annually in Puerto Rico [is] 17,000. This implies that approximately one out of every five women who get pregnant obtains an abortion" (5). According to the Pro Mujer study, reasons for choosing an abortion are as follows:

> The three most common reasons are: the financial difficulties they will face if they have a baby (68%), the difficulties in assuming more responsibilities (68%), and child care problems (57%). Most of the women surveyed did not want to get pregnant and may already had all the children they wanted to have (36%), or considered themselves too old to bear children (9%). Other women believed that the most responsible decision was to put off having children until they had a better relationship with their partners (33%) or until they were older (28%). Others wanted to have children but had serious health problems (12%), or knew of or feared serious abnormalities in the fetus (29%), or had other personal problems (24%) (9).

These numbers lend support to several possibilities. One is that Puerto Rican women in Puerto Rico generally accept motherhood as their defining role, in that 68% cited financial difficulties. On the other hand 68% did not want to assume more responsibilities and 57% cited child care problems. This could indicate a valuing of self-determination and personal goals, but this is ambiguous. To explore this further, I telephoned one of the researchers on this project, "Alice," who conducted each of the "six to eight" personal interviews with abortion patients in this study. Speaking from memory (not transcription or notes), she described several narratives. One involved a women who was "having problems" with her husband; another involved a married woman who wanted to finish her studies; and several involved coping with abandonment. Alice found the women coping with abandonment to be the most "remorseful." Summarizing her interviews, she said that the abortions were "voluntary, and the woman was generally happy with the decision and would do it again."

An article about the Pro Mujer study (Muniz 1992) was featured in *Instantes*, the newsletter of the Latina Initiative, Catholics for a Free Choice. The same issue contained a profile of a co-director, Luis Alberto Aviles. In her description of how working on the study affected Aviles, Claudia Lopez Muniz explained that he "came to see that the abortion decision is more than economics. Especially in Puerto Rico, he says, the day-to-day responsibilities and the social and emotional costs of raising a family are not shared. They fall primarily on the mothers, many of whom are single parents"(5). Aviles explained how his participation in the abortion study changed him: "I began to make the connections among feminism, health, and politics. And I realized that abortion politics are politics of control -- gender politics (5-6).

The comments of Judith, Alice, and Luis Aviles indicate that gender is an issue in Puerto Rico, and that some Puerto Ricans are challenging the idea that an acceptance of male-centered values is intrinsic to being Puerto Rican.

This research has analyzed how the experience of aborting a pregnancy can undermine the virginity-marriage-motherhood and the bounded sexuality-motherhood plots that form the patriarchal cultural story. Undermining patriarchy is, of course, the project of the feminist movement. I would like to end with Cherrie Moraga's insightful account of her coming to terms with her Chicana culture and family life, and her lesbianism. In her essay, "From a Long Line of *Vendidas* [Traitors]: Chicanas and Feminism" (1986), she describes an alienation from her family and her culture that echoes what some of the women I interviewed told me. She explains that, when she was a teenager, her light skin allowed her to "pass" as an anglo, and that she took advantage of this out of longing for personal and sexual freedom:

> I did not move away from other Chicanos because I did not love my people. I gradually became anglocized because I thought it was the only option available to me toward gaining autonomy as a person without being sexually stigmatized. I can't say that I was conscious of all this at the time, only that at each juncture in my development, I instinctively made choices which I thought would allow me greater freedom of movement in the future. This primarily meant resisting sex roles as

much as I could safely manage and this was far easier in an anglo context than in a Chicano one. That is not to say that anglo culture does not
stigmatize its women for 'gender-transgressions' -- only that its stigma-
tizing did not hold the personal power over me which Chicano culture
did (174).

Eventually Moraga became part of the feminist movement and the
movement for Chicano liberation and identified herself as a Chicana
lesbian feminist. Although she believes that family life can be a source
of strength, she is critical of the sexism within the Chicano liberation
movement, especially its unexamined valuing of family life:

> The family, then, becomes all the more ardently protected by oppressed
> peoples, and the sanctity of the institution is infused like blood into the
> veins of the Chicano. At all costs, la familia must be preserved. ... So we
> fight back, we think, with our families -- with our women pregnant, and
> our men the indisputable heads. We believe the more severely we pro-
> tect the sex roles within the family, the stronger we will be as a unit in
> opposition to the anglo threat. And yet, our refusal to examine all the
> roots of the lovelessness in our families is our weakest link and softest
> spot (181).

Moraga's resolution of the conflict between women's well-being and the
importance of familial interdependence is one that would be appreci-
ated, I think, by many of the women who participated in this research. I
cannot improve upon her eloquence, so I will give her the last word:

> Family is not by definition the man in a dominant position over women
> and children. Familia is cross-generational bonding, deep emotional ties
> between opposite sexes, and within our sex. It is sexuality, which in-
> volves, but is not limited to, intercourse or orgasm. It springs forth from
> touch, constant and daily. The ritual of kissing and the sign of the cross
> with every coming and going from the home. It is finding familia
> among friends where blood ties are formed through suffering and cele-
> bration shared. The strength of our families never came from domina-
> tion. It has only endured in spite of it -- like our women (182).

Appendixes

Appendix A:
Looking for Members of a Hidden Population

The data analyzed in this study are the results of two kinds of research, personal interviews and focus groups. During 1991 and 1992 I conducted personal interviews with twenty Puerto Rican women living in the Chicago area who have had an abortion. Each interview was conducted in English at a location chosen by the respondent, either her home, her workplace, or a restaurant. Interviews lasted between one and two hours. They were tape recorded and written up afterward as a combination of notes and transcription.

Using a semi-structured interview guide (Appendix B), I asked each woman if she had imagined what her life would be like if she continued the pregnancy and if she got an abortion. I also asked about how her life had progressed since then, her plans for the future, her religious beliefs, her relationship with the man with whom she got pregnant, her parents and other family members. During the interview I asked follow-up, or "probe" questions at appropriate points, to elicit further information (Lofland and Lofland 1984:53-62). In general, I have used the methodological practices, e.g. coding for common themes, simultaneous analysis and data collection, and analytical memos, outlined by Lofland and Lofland (1984). I have analyzed the completed interviews for common patterns and themes. This analysis indicates the gender strategies (Hochschild 1991) each woman uses to negotiate her beliefs about gender, her upbringing, and the social situation in which she finds herself.

I have focused my research on Puerto Rican women rather than Latinas in general because my sample is small and I don't want to confound cultural differences between Puerto Rican women and other Latinas with other variables. Additionally, I do not speak Spanish and according to both personal and published sources (e.g. Rodriguez 1991) Puerto Ricans are more likely than other Latinas to be fluent in English.

Given the shame and secrecy that surround the issue of abortion, locating Puerto Rican women willing to be interviewed has been difficult. I relied on an extensive network of women working in health and social service agencies and academic settings in the Chicago area. I also placed a "personal" advertisement in the *Extra*, a bi-lingual newspaper, for five weeks, which read: "If you are a Puerto Rican woman over eighteen and you have had an abortion, I would like to talk to you for my research. The interview will be completely private and I will not use your name. Please call Jean at (my phone number)."

Over a period of eighteen months, I developed a network of twenty-six women who agreed to try and find respondents for my Study. Some of them used their personal networks and others cooperated with me as part of their employment. Women in the second category work at an abortion clinic, a center for teen mothers, an infant mortality reduction center, a hospital clinic, and a neighborhood health clinic. Some of these facilities are in Puerto Rican neighborhoods while others have a diverse clientele. One woman put up fliers in a neighborhood health clinic and a local branch of the public library. I have had informant interviews (8) with the women I am working with at each site.

Of these twenty-six women, only five were able to find at least one respondent. Seven (of twenty) respondents were located this way, through an intermediary. Only one of these respondents was a client or a patient. The other six were family members, co-workers, former students, or friends. Seven women (of the twenty-six) offered to be respondents themselves. Five respondents were located with the "personal" ad. One responded to the flier at the neighborhood health clinic. The names (pseudonyms) and demographic characteristics of the respondents are charted in Appendix C. In recruiting respondents and conducting the interviews, I have followed the procedures required for the protection of human subjects: assuring each respondent of confidentiality, assuring each respondent that her interview is voluntary and that she may refuse to answer any question or terminate the interview, and confining my respondents to adult women over eighteen.

I suspect that some of the women who wanted to help me found themselves unable to ask another woman if she would be willing to talk about her abortion. My difficulty in locating respondents and conversations with other informants suggest this. Ten women who quoted refusals to me said they were told that "I don't want to talk about it," or "it's too painful." Some women, including a high school teacher, a high school social worker, and health care personnel, did not have anyone in mind to ask, but offered to be alert to interview possibilities for me.

In contrast to the difficult and time consuming process just described, I was able to get the names and telephone numbers of fifty-two white women who had abortions at a Chicago area abortion clinic within a three month period in 1989 (Peterman 1990). When I began the present research, I expected to be able to use a similar procedure for Puerto Rican women. My intention was to enlist several (three or four) clinic workers and the like and ask them to try and find clients or patients willing to be interviewed. After about six months, it became obvious that this strategy was unproductive and I began to expand my network to eventually include twenty-six women.

My difficulty in locating Puerto Rican women to be interviewed is consistent with the experience of Cannon, Higgenbotham, and Leung (1988), who found that women who volunteer as research subjects are most likely to be middle class and white. Women of color and women who are poor often know little about how research is done, are concerned about anonymity, and face structural problems such as lack of free time. Cannon, Higginbotham, and Leung state that more labor intensive strategies, involving personal contact, are necessary in order to involve women of color. One Puerto Rican woman I interviewed told the person who asked her about being interviewed that she wanted to meet me before she decided whether or not she would allow me to interview her.

The three recruitment modes — direct contact, contact through an intermediary, and contact through a newspaper ad or posted flier — were somewhat correlated with how respondents experienced their abortions. The narratives of the direct contact respondents tend to be empowerment stories. That is, getting an abortion allowed them to remain in school or leave unsatisfactory relationships. The narratives of women who responded to the personal ad or the posted flier tend to be recovery stories. These narratives are about male abandonment or betrayal of some kind. The narratives of women who were contacted through an intermediary are some of each, though leaning towards empowerment.

Each of the twenty interviewees is part of a hidden population, Puerto Rican women who have had an abortion. As a hidden population, their characteristics are unknown, and there is no way to determine to what extent these interviewees "represent" Puerto Rican women who have had abortions. Their educational and occupational attainments suggest that they are better off economically than the local Puerto Rican population in general, which is characterized by a 31.6% poverty rate in Cook County (Robles 1988). Their higher economic status is consistent with the fact that, for many women, including more than half of my sample, getting an abortion allows the woman to maintain opportunity for herself, either by staying in school or remaining employed. Additionally, a self-selection factor may be operating as well. Women who volunteer for a research interview may be more self-confident, or more economically successful that others. The usefulness of this research does not rest on any claim to "represent" Puerto Rican women or Puerto Rican women who get abortions. Rather, it rests on an accurate interpretation of the narratives and the extent to which this interpretation is consistent with (as well as goes beyond) what is already known about Puerto Rican life.

Another part of this project consisted of two focus groups (group interviews). Each of these groups was composed of women who worked together or attended school together. Each group met with me once for a period of about one and a half hours, and each session was tape recorded. One group consisted of twelve young women in their late teens, and the other consisted of six women between twenty-one and thirty-four. Participants in the first group are students at an alternative high school, and participants in the second group staff a Head Start program. In each group, I asked participants to talk about what they learned while growing up about how a Puerto Rican woman should behave with respect to relationships, sex, marriage, and children, how this fit (or didn't fit) their later experience, and if their beliefs have changed. I also asked if they think they could talk to their mothers about birth control and abortion and if they think their daughters could talk to them.

I gained access to the focus group participants in the same manner as to the respondents, through networks and asking around. The principal of the alternative high school was very supportive of my research, and decided to give female students one fourth of a credit hour for their participation. These teenagers and young women were excitable and animated. They were both proud and critical of their Puerto Rican heritage. Some had strong opinions for and against contraception and abortion. Fortunately, a university student from one of my classes was able to assist me with this focus group by taking notes and keeping track of who was speaking. This university student is Puerto Rican and her presence may have helped bridge any barrier between me and the high school students.

The second focus group was smaller and its participants were older. I conducted this session without an assistant, because I was unable to locate one. However, the pace of the discussion, while animated, was slower than the earlier one, and I was able to take adequate notes myself. In both groups, I asked each participant to print her first name on a card to be placed in front of her, so I could keep track of who was speaking.

My purpose in conducting the focus groups was to gain some insight into Puerto Rican culture. I wanted to learn more about what Richardson (1990) calls the cultural story about what it means to be a Puerto Rican woman, as part of the context for the interviews about abortion. In addition to this cultural story, the focus groups also elicited what Richardson calls the collective story of resistance, in this case, to male dominance.

As a white, middle class researcher outside the culture of the women I interviewed, I sometimes felt my otherness keenly. On the other hand, my informants and interviewees took care of me, often without my asking, by explaining aspects of Puerto Rican culture they thought I needed to know. One informant stated that it would be unlikely that a Puerto Rican would do a study like this one because the idea of talking about abortion would be viewed so negatively by some members of her family and others close to her.

Several strategies have been helpful in familiarizing myself with the local Puerto Rican community and Puerto Rican culture in general. The informant interviews and focus groups have been especially helpful. I have conducted respondent interviews in the woman's home or a neighborhood restaurant whenever possible. I have almost always used a combination of public transportation and walking, which allowed me to observe the neighborhood and take brief field notes. Early in this study I discovered that fiction (in English) by Puerto Rican writers (Cofer 1989; Ferre 1991, 1995; Gomez, Moraga and Romo-Carmona 1983; Mohr 1985, 1986; de Monteflores 1989; Morales and Morales 1986; Turner 1991; and Velez 1988) provides an immersion into Puerto Rican culture that narrowly focused academic studies often lack.

One of my informants, Laura (a pseudonym), who is especially supportive of my research invited me and another Anglo friend of hers to attend the Puerto Rican Parade and Festival in June of 1991. Such festivals only skim the surface of a particular culture. Nevertheless, they can provide an enjoyable introduction. Watching the parade provided a sense of the bi-cultural nature of the Puerto Rican community and its political clout. Floats and marching groups included the following: a major drug store chain, a furniture store, banks, realtors, the phone company, the Chicago Police Department, the Kelvin Park High School Band, the Wells Academy Band, organizations representing various towns in Puerto Rico, numerous beauty queens, and an AIDS awareness group which passed out condoms to onlookers. Politicians who marched in the parade included both government officials from Puerto Rico and Chicago office holders. Mayor Daley was wearing a *guayabuera* (Puerto Rican style shirt). A woman standing near me was talking back to some of the floats as they passed, and Laura translated some of her Spanish, e.g. "your prices are too high," and "why did you give me a ticket?" The bi-cultural nature of the event was captured in one of the many T-shirts for sale. The shirt featured a picture of Bart Simpson wearing a Puerto Rican flag as his shirt. The caption read "Let's salsa! Viva Puerto Rico!"

After the parade we went to Humboldt Park for the Puerto Rican Festival, a three day event. The overwhelming first impression was one of cars, honking horns, and Puerto Rican flags being waved from car windows. This giant Puerto Rican traffic jam seemed essential to the festival. Like most other ethnic groups (Bakalian 1993) Puerto Ricans consider their food to be a distinctive and important component of ethnicity. Puerto Rican food was abundant at the festival. With Laura's guidance, I enjoyed watermelon juice, *arroz con gandules* (rice with pigeon peas), and fried bananas.

On another occasion Laura and I were shopping and she showed me the ingredients for *arroz con gandules*, promising to call me with the recipe. She called her mother, who lives in Puerto Rico, and then called me with her mother's recipe. Several minutes later, Laura called again, saying that her mother had called to say that she had forgotten the olive oil. I was touched by Laura's mother's pride in her cooking and her concern that I get it right.

In spite of the general reluctance to talk about abortion that made finding respondents so difficult, I sensed a concern that I get it right in most of the people involved in the study. Women who agreed to be interviewed, and other people who helped me, seemed to be pleased that someone was studying Puerto Ricans, and giving them voice. One of the high school focus group participants expressed her belief about how non-Puerto Ricans think about people like her. She said

> We get underestimated a lot. We'll never make it. We have babies. But I walk with my head up high 'cause I don't care [what they think]. If you're a young Puerto Rican teenage mother, they put you down.

At the end of the session, when I asked her group for any final thoughts, this same young woman responded, "Puerto Rican women are capable of anything."

Appendix B:
Interview Guide

I would like you to look back on your abortion experience. These questions are to help you think about it, and feel free to add any other information that you want.

Before we start, I want to assure you that this interview is confidential and that your name will not be used. If I bring up anything you don't want to talk about, just say you don't want to talk about it. You may stop the interview at any time.

With your permission I'd like to tape the interview. The tapes will not be transcribed. I will use them to check my notes.

First, I must verify that you are an adult. Are you at least 18 years old?

A. Would you tell me what your life was like shortly before you realized that you were pregnant?

1. Were you in school?
(What did you think about school?)
(What were your grades?)
(What did you think about your grades?)
(Did you have plans for further education?)

2. Were you employed?
(Did you like your job?)
(Did you think you had opportunities for advancement at your job?)
(Was the income from your job adequate for you to support yourself?)
(How did you support yourself financially?)

3. Who were you living with? (husband, family, boyfriend, roommate)
Did members of this household get along?
Did you get along with the members of this household?

4. Tell me about your friends.

5. In general, how would you describe your life at that time?

6. How long ago was this?

B. I'd like to ask you some questions about the kinds of help and support you got when you discovered that you were pregnant.

1. Who knew about your pregnancy? Did your (parents, partner or husband, sisters or brothers, relatives, friends) know?

For the remainder of this section encourage respondent to discuss each relevant person.

2. Did you tell them?

3. What was their reaction to your pregnancy?

4. Did any of them help you to decide whether or not to get an abortion? (How?)

5. Do you know how each of them feels about your decision to get the abortion? (describe)

6. Is it important to you that each of them agree with your decision?

7. At the time you decided to get your abortion, did you know anyone who had gotten one?

C. Now I'd like to ask you about how you made your decision.

1. As you were deciding what to do, did you think about what your life would be like if you did not get an abortion?
(What did you think about?)
(How did you feel about this?)

2. As you were deciding what to do, did you think about what your life would be like if you got an abortion?
(What did you think about?)
(How did you feel about this?)

3. What are the two or three main reasons that you decided to get an abortion?

4. Is there another reason?

5. Do you think your decision to get an abortion changed you in any way? (How?)

6. Would you describe the decision as difficult?
(Why?)

7. Do you think you have made other decisions in your life as significant as your decision to get an abortion?
(How do they compare to the abortion decision?)

8. If you could arrange things just the way you wanted, what would you like to be doing right now?

9. Have you thought about what you would like your life to be like about five years from now? (describe)

10. How did you find the place where you got the abortion? (i.e. phone book, referral, friend or relative)

D. Take me back to the day when you got your abortion.

1. What was going through your mind?

2. Do you remember any conversations you had that day?

3. Did anyone go with you when you got your abortion?
(Who?)

4. Were you met at or near the clinic by any person or group who tried to talk you out of it?
(How did you feel about this?)

5. What was going through your mind after the abortion was over?

E. These questions are about the relationship that existed with your (husband/boyfriend) at the time you were pregnant.

1. How long had you been in that relationship?

2. Would you describe the relationship as "serious?"

3. Were you using contraception?

4. Are you still in that relationship?

(Do you think the relationship is stronger now, weaker, or about the same?)
            or

(When did the relationship end?)
(Do you think that the pregnancy or the abortion had anything to do with the end of the relationship?)

5. How do you feel about this relationship?

F. Tell me a little about what your life is like now.

    1. Are you in school?
  (What do you think about school?)
  (What are your grades?)
  (What do you think about your grades?)
  (Do you have plans for further education?)

    2. Are you employed?
  (Do you like your job?)
  (Do you think you have opportunities for advancement
  at your job?)
  (Is the income from your job adequate for you to support yourself?)
  (How do you support yourself financially?)

    3. Who are you living with? (husband, family, boyfriend, roommate)
  Do members of this household get along?
  Do you get along with the members of this household?

    4. Tell me about your friends.

    5. In general, how would you describe your life now?

    6. How would you describe yourself?

G. Now I'd like to ask you a some questions about your background and your personal beliefs.

    1. Were you born in Puerto Rico? (Or in the U.S.?)

    2. How long have you lived in the U.S.?

    3. Do you go to Puerto Rico?
  (How often?)
  (How long do you stay?)
  (Do you visit family?)

    4. Do you associate more with Puerto Ricans or with North Americans?

    5. Do you speak both Spanish and English?
  (When do you speak Spanish?)
  (When do you speak English?)

    6. Before you got pregnant, did you have an opinion about abortion?
  (What was it?)

    7. Has your experience changed your opinion about abortion?

(In what way?)

8. Do you think you made the right decision about your pregnancy?

9. Do you know if your parents have an opinion about abortion?
(What does each of them think about it?)

10. If a close friend of yours came to you for advice because she was pregnant and didn't know what to do, what would you tell her?

11. Was this your first abortion?

(Can you remember what your life was like shortly before you got your first abortion?)

(Can you remember how you made that decision, what you thought about, who you talk to, who helped you?)

12. I'm going to read four statements. After I read each one, just tell me if you agree or disagree with the statement.

I. It is much better for everyone if the man is the achiever and the woman takes care of the home and family.
Agree   Disagree

II. It is more important for a wife to help her husband's career or job than to have one herself.
Agree   Disagree

III. A working mother can establish just as warm and secure a relationship with her children as a mother who does not work.
Agree   Disagree

IV. A preschool child is likely to suffer if his or her mother works.
Agree   Disagree

What are your feelings, in general, about these statements?

13. Do you have any children?
(How many?)

14. Were you raised in a particular religion? (which?)

15. Do you consider yourself _____ today?
(If not, do you consider yourself a member of another religion?)

(16. Do you know if (your religion) takes a position on abortion? What is it?)

(17. If you think your church would disapprove of your abortion, how do you feel about this?)

(18. How important is your religion [or your relationship to God] to you? Would you say it is very important, somewhat important, or not very important?)

19. Which three of these are most important to you?

friends	job
money	boyfriend/husband
family	children
self	happiness
	health

Can you explain why?

20. What is your date of birth?

21. Is there anything you would like to add, or anything that you would like to ask me?

22. May I call you again if I have another question to ask you?

That's all. Thank you very much.

Appendix C: Characteristics of Interviewees

Name	Age at Interview	Age at Abortion	Married or Live-in	Children	Religion	Told
Felice	36	16	no	one	none	partner
Lydia	41	32	married	two	Catholic	partner
Caroline	58	21	no	one	none	sister-in-law
Lucy	26	18	no	four	Catholic	mother
Miriam	29	19	married	no	none	partner
Lupe	27	15	no	no	none	no one
Julia	24	15	live-in	six	none	no one
Marisol	31	31	no	two	Catholic	partner
Mayra	37	19	married	two	Catholic	partner
Carmen	43	20	no	four	Catholic	no one
Alicia	32	23	no	two	none	partner
Diana	31	30	no	no	none	partner
Evelyn	31	18	no	no	none	partner
Mercedes	26	21	married	two	Catholic	partner
Helena	49	37	married	six	none	partner
Cherrie	42	36	married	one	Baptist	partner
Sylvia	21	18	married	one	none	mother and partner
Rosa	26	17	live-in	no	none	partner
Gloria	31	25	no	no	none	partner
Ana	29	24	no	four	none	partner

Name	Decision Difficult	Meaning*	Education	Occupation or Source of Support
Felice	yes	keeping	some college	social worker
Lydia	no	keeping	high school	abortion counselor
Caroline	no	control	some college	social worker
Lucy	no	keeping	assoc. deg.	bookkeeper
Miriam	no	keeping	Ph.D.	college professor
Lupe	no	keeping	college	high school teacher
Julia	no	keeping	drop-out	public aid
Marisol	yes	keeping and abandon	drop-out	store manager
Mayra	no	keeping	some college	disability
Carmen	no	control	some college	health advocate
Alicia	yes	keeping	college	social worker
Diana	yes	keeping	college	student
Evelyn	yes	keeping	master's candidate	student
Mercedes	yes	abandon	unknown	social worker
Helena	yes	health	unknown	public relations
Cherrie	yes	abandon	some college	quality control
Sylvia	yes	control and abandon	drop-out	homemaker
Rosa	yes	keeping and control	some nursing	manufacturing
Gloria	yes	abandon	college	insurance
Ana	yes	abandon	drop-out	public aid

*Meanings: "keeping on being who I was" (keeping); preserving life or health (health); coping with physical or emotional abandonment (coping); resisting or escaping male control (control).

Bibliography

Addelson, Kathryn Pyne 1991. *Impure Thoughts: Essays on Philosophy, Feminism, and Ethics*. Philadelphia: Temple University Press.

Amaro, Hortensia 1982. "Psychological Determinants of Abortion Attitudes Among Mexican-American Women," Ph.D. dissertation, Department of Psychology, U.C.L.A.

Amott, Teresa 1993. *Caught in the Crisis: Women and the U.S. Economy Today*. New York: Cornerstone Books, an imprint of Monthly Review Press.

Anderson, Elijah 1990. *Streetwise: Race, Class and Change in an Urban Community*. Chicago and London: University of Chicago Press.

Avakian, Arlene Voski 1988. "Introduction: Tradition and Resistance to Tradition," *Ararat, Special Feminist Issue* XXIX: 2-8.

Azize, Yamila and Luis A. Aviles 1993. *Abortion in Puerto Rico: Current Practice and Policy Recommendations*. Women's Studies Project, Cayey University College, University of Puerto Rico.

Badillo, David 1992. "Latinos and Catholicism: Challenging the Sacred Cow," University of Illinois at Chicago, Chicago Studies Program, Office of Social Science Research Speakers Series.

Bakalian, Anny P. 1992. *Armenian-Americans: From Being to Feeling Armenian*. New Brunswick: Transaction Publishers.

Blanchard, Dallas A. and Terry J. Prewitt, 1993. *Religious Violence and Abortion: The Gideon Project*. Gainesville: University Press of Florida.

Bonavoglia, Angela, ed. 1991. *The Choices We Made: Twenty-Five Women and Men Speak Out About Abortion*. New York: Random House.

Burgos, Nilsa M. and Yolanda I. Diaz Perez 1986. "An Exploration of Human Sexuality in the Puerto Rican Culture," *Journal of Social Work and Human Sexuality* 4:135-150.

Callahan, Sidney and Daniel Callahan, eds. 1984. *Abortion: Understanding Differences*. New York: Plenum Press.

Campbell Anne 1984. *The Girls in the Gang: A Report from New York City*. New York: Basil Blackwell.

Cannon, Lynn Weber, Elizabeth Higginbotham, and Marianne L. A. Leung 1988. "Race and Class Bias in Qualitative Research on Women," *Gender and Society* 2: 449-462.

Casuso, Jorge and Eduardo Camacho 1989. *Hispanics in Chicago*. Chicago: The Chicago Reporter and the Center for Community Research and Assistance of the Community Renewal Society.

Chicago Abused Women Coalition, undated. "Chicago Abused Women."

Christ, Carol P. 1980. *Diving Deep and Surfacing: Women Writers on a Spiritual Quest*. Boston: Beacon Press.

Cofer, Judith Ortiz 1990. *Silent Dancing: A Partial Remembrance of a Puerto Rican Childhood*. Houston: Arte Publico Press.

_____ 1989. *The Line of the Sun*. Athens and London: The University of Georgia Press.

Connections: An International Women's Quarterly 1990. (no author), "When Does a Law Work Too Well?" 34: 20-21.

Crane, Jonathan 1991. "The Epidemic Theory of Ghettos and Neighborhood Effects on Dropping Out and Teenage Childbearing," *American Journal of Sociology* 96:1226-1259.

Degler, Carl N. 1985. *Out of Our Past: The Forces that Shaped Modern America*. New York: Harper Colophon Books.

Enloe, Cynthia 1989. *Bananas, Beaches, and Bases: Making Feminist Sense of International Politics*. Berkeley: University of California Press.

Erickson, Victoria Lee 1993. *Where Silence Speaks: Feminism, Social Theory and Religion*. Minneapolis: Fortress Press.

Espin, Olivia M. 1984. "Cultural and Historical Influences on Sexuality in Hispanic/Latin Women: Implications for Psychotherapy," in Carole Vance, ed., *Pleasure and Danger: Exploring Female Sexuality*. Boston: Routledge and Kegan Paul.

Ferre, Rosario 1991. *The Youngest Doll*. Lincoln and London: University of Nebraska Press.

_____ 1995. *The House on the Lagoon*. New York: Farrar, Strauss and Giroux.

Forrest, Jacqueline Darroch and Susheela Singh 1990. "The Sexual and Reproductive Behavior of American Women, 1982-1988" *Family Planning Perspectives*. 22: 206-214.

Forrest, Jacqueline Darroch and Stanley K. Henshaw 1987. "The Harassment of U.S. Abortion Providers," *Family Planning Perspectives* 19:9-13.

Friedman, Jennifer 1992. "Pathways to Adulthood for Latina and White Adolescents and the Role of the Family," *Latino Studies Journal* 3: 9-30.

Garcia-Preto, Nydia 1982. "Puerto Rican Families," in Monica McGoldrick, John K. Pearce, and Joseph Giodano, eds., *Ethnicity and Family Therapy*. New York: The Guilford Press.

Giachello, Aida and Idalia Torres 1993. "Maternal and Perinatal Issues of Latino Women in the United States," in Carlos Molinas, Pedro Lecca, and Marilyn Molinas, eds., *Health Status of Latinos in the United States*, Washington, D.C: American Public Health Association.

Gilbarg, Dan and Luis M. Falcon 1993. "Latinos in the Labor Market: Mexicans, Puerto Ricans, and Cubans," *Latino Studies Journal* III: 60-87.

Gilligan, Carol, 1982. *In a Different Voice*. Cambridge: Harvard University Press.

Gluck, Sherna Berger and Daphne Patai 1991. *Practice of Oral History*. New York and London: Routledge.

Gomez, Alma, Cherrie Moraga and Mariana Romo-Carmona 1983. *Cuentos: Stories by Latinas*. Latham NY: Kitchen Table Women of Color Press.

Gordon, Linda 1977. *Woman's Body, Woman's Right: A History of Birth Control in America*. New York: Penguin.

_____ 1982. "Why Nineteenth-Century Feminists Did Not Support `Birth Control' and Twentieth Century Feminists Do: Feminism, Reproduction, and the Family," in Barrie Thorne and Marilyn Yalom, eds. *Rethinking the Family: Some Feminist Questions*. New York: Longman.

_____1986. "Why is Reproductive Choice So Controversial? An Historical Perspective," Speech given at Funders' Briefing on Reproductive Rights and Reproductive Health, Chicago.

Granberg, Donald and Beth Wellman Granberg, 1980. "Abortion Attitudes, 1965-1980: Trends and Determinants" *Family Planning Perspectives* 12:250-261.

Gross, David M., and Sophfronia Scott 1990. "Proceeding With Caution", *Time*, July 16.

Harris, Louis 1990. "Supreme Court Webster Decision Produces Backlash Against Anti-Abortion Cause." New York: Louis Harris and Associates.

Harrison, Beverly Wildung 1983. *Our Right to Choose: Toward a New Ethic of Abortion*. Boston: Beacon Press.

Hartmann, Betsy 1987. *Reproductive Rights and Wrongs: The Global Politics of Population Control and Contraceptive Choice*. New York: Harper and Row.

Heilbrun, Carolyn G. 1979. *Reinventing Womanhood*. New York: W.W. Norton and Co.

_____ 1988. *Writing a Woman's Life*. New York: Ballatine Books.

Henshaw, Stanley K. and Jane Silverman 1988. "The Characteristics and Prior Contraceptive Use of U.S. Abortion Patients," *Family Planning Perspectives* 20: 158-168.

Hochschild, Arlie, with Anne Machung 1989. *The Second Shift: Working Parents and the Revolution at Home*. New York: Viking.

hooks, bell 1984. *Feminist Theory: from margin to center*. Boston: South End Press.

_____ 1989. *Talking Back: thinking feminist, thinking black*. Boston: South End Press.

Horowitz, Ruth 1983. *Honor and the American Dream: Culture and Identity in a Chicano Community*. New Brunswick NJ: Rutgers University Press.

Howe, Louise Kapp 1984. *Moments on Maple Avenue: The Reality of Abortion.* New York: Warner Books.

Illinois Coalition Against Domestic Violence, undated. "Illinois Domestic Violence Act: Finally ... relief for victims of the hidden crime."

Jargowsky, Paul A. and Mary Jo Bane 1990. "Neighborhood Poverty: Basic Questions." Discussion Paper Series, #H-90-3, Malcolm Wiener Center for Social Policy, John F. Kennedy School of Government, Harvard University, Cambridge, MA.

Kandiyoti, Deniz 1988. "Bargaining With Patriarchy," *Gender and Society* 2: 274-290.

Klein, Ethel 1984. *Gender Politics: From Consciousness to Mass Politics.* Cambridge: Harvard University Press.

Lerner, Gerda 1993. *The Creation of Feminist Consciousness: From the Middle Ages to Eighteen-Seventy.* New York: Oxford University Press.

Lofland, John and Lyn H. Lofland 1984. *Analyzing Social Settings: A Guide to Qualitative Observation and Analysis.* Belmont California: Wadsworth Publishing Co.

Luker, Kristin 1977. *Taking Chances: Abortion and the Decision Not to Contracept.* Berkeley: University of California Press.

_____ 1984. *Abortion and the Politics of Motherhood,* Berkeley: University of California Press.

Maguire, Daniel C. 1983. "Abortion: A Question of Catholic Honesty." *The Christian Century* Sept. 14-21: 803-807.

Martin, Biddy and Chandra Talpade Mohanty 1986. "Feminist Politics: What's Home Got to Do With It?", in Teresa de Laurentis, ed. *Feminist Studies, Critical Studies.* Bloomington: Indiana University Press.

Mason, Karen and Yu-Hsia Lu 1988. "Attitudes Toward Women's Familial Roles: Changes in the United States, 1977-1985. *Gender and Society* 2: 39-57.

Messer, Ellen and Kathryn May, 1988. *Back Rooms: Voices From the Illegal Abortion Era.* New York: St. Martin's.

Miller, Patricia G. 1993. *The Worst of Times: Illegal Abortion -- Survivors, Practitioners, Coroners, Cops, and Children of Women Who Died Talk About its Horrors.* New York: Harper Collins.

Mohr, James C. 1978. *Abortion in America: The Origins and Evolution of National Policy, 1800-1900.* New York: Oxford University Press.

Mohr, Nicholasa 1985. *Rituals of Survival: A Woman's Portfolio.* Houston: Arte Publico Press.

_____ 1986. *El Bronx Remembered.* Houston: Arte Publico Press.

de Monteflores, Carmen 1989. *Singing Softly.* San Francisco: spinsters/aunt lute.

Moraga, Cherrie, and Gloria Anzaldua 1981. *This Bridge Called My Back: Writings by Radical Women of Color.* Watertown, Ma: Persephone Press.

_____ 1986. "From a Long Line of *Vendidas*: Chicanas and Feminism" in Teresa
    de Laurentis, ed. *Feminist Studies, Critical Studies*. Bloomington: Indiana
    University Press.
Morales, Aurora Levins and Rosario Morales 1986. *Getting Home Alive*.
    Ithaca, New York: Firebrand Books.
Muniz, Claudia Lopez 1992. "Results of Abortion Study in Puerto Rico,"
    Instantes, newsletter of Latina Initiative, Catholics for a Free Choice 1:5,6.
National Opinion Research Center 1988. *General Social Surveys, 1972-1988:
    Cumulative Codebook*. University of Chicago.
Noelle-Neumann, Elizabeth 1974. "The Spiral of Silence: A Theory of Public
    Opinion," *Journal of Communication* 24: 43-51.
Noonan, John T. Jr. ed., 1970. *The Morality of Abortion: Legal and Historical
    Perspectives*. Cambridge: Harvard University Press.
Northeast Project on Latina Women and Reproductive Health, in collaboration
    with Women of Color Partnership Program, Religious Coalition for
    Abortion Rights Educational Fund, Inc, 1991. *Puertorriquenas: Reproductive
    Health and Sociodemographics Among Puerto Rican Women in the U.S.:
    A Fact Handbook.* (Hartford, CN).
Padilla, Felix M. 1985. *Latino Ethnic Consciousness: The Case of Mexican
    Americans and Puerto Ricans in Chicago*. South Bend, Indiana: University of
    Notre Dame Press.
Parsons, Kathryn Pyne 1978. "Moral Revolution," in Julia A. Sherman and
    Evelyn Torton Beck, eds., *The Prism of Sex: Essays in the Sociology of
    Knowledge*. Madison: The University of Wisconsin Press.
Personal Narratives Group 1989. *Interpreting Women's Lives: Feminist Theory and
    Personal Narratives*. Bloomington and Indianapolis: Indiana University
    Press.
Petchesky, Rosalind Pollack, 1985. *Abortion and Women's Choice: The State,
    Sexuality and Reproductive Freedom*, Boston: Northeastern University Press.
_____ 1987. "Fetal Images: The Power of Visual Culture in the Politics of
    Reproduction," *Feminist Studies* 13: 263-292.
Peterman, Jean 1990. "The Abortion Decision: Women Tell Their Stories,"
    master's paper, Department of Sociology, University of Illinois at Chicago.
_____ 1993. "Puerto Rican Women Deciding to Get an Abortion: Beginning a
    Collective Story," *Latino Studies Journal Special Issue on Latina Women*.4:44-59.
Plutzer, Eric, 1988. "Work Life, Family Life and Women's Support of
    Feminism," *American Sociological Review* 53:640-649.
Ramirez de Arellano, Annette B. and Conrad Seipp 1983. *Colonialism,
    Catholicism, and Contraception: A History of Birth Control in Puerto Rico*.
    Chapel Hill: University of North Carolina Press.
Rich, Adrienne 1979. *On Lies, Secrets, and Silence: Selected Prose 1966-1978*.
    New York: W. W. Norton and Co.

Richardson, Laurel 1990. "Narrative and Sociology," *Journal of Contemporary Ethnography* 19: 116-135.

Rios, Palmira N. 1990. "Export-Oriented Industrialization and the Demand for Female Labor: Puerto Rican Women in the Manufacturing Sector, 1952-1980," *Gender and Society* 4: 321-337.

Robles, Jennifer Juarez 1988. "Hispanics Emerging as Nation's Poorest Minority Group," *Chicago Reporter* 17(6): 1, 8-9.

Rodriguez, Clara E. 1991. *Puerto Ricans: Born in the U.S.A.* Boulder, San Francisco, Oxford: Westview Press (first published 1989, Unwin and Hyman).

Rothman, Barbara Katz 1989. *Recreating Motherhood: Ideology and Technology in Patriarchal Society,* New York: W. W. Norton & Co.

Russo, Ann 1991. " 'We Cannot Live Without Our Lives': White Women, Anti-racism, and Feminism," in Chandra Mohanty, Ann Russo, and Lourdes Tor res, eds.,*Third World Women and the Politics of Feminism.* Bloomington: Indi ana University Press.

Say, Elizabeth 1990. *Evidence on Her Own Behalf: Women's Narratives as Theological Voice.* Savage Md: Rowman and Littlefield.

Scott, Jacqueline and Howard Schuman 1988. "Attitude Strength and Social Action in the Abortion Dispute," *American Sociological Review* 53:785-793.

Smith-Rosenberg, Carroll 1985. *Disorderly Conduct: Visions of Gender in Victorian America.* New York: Alfred A. Knopf.

Solinger, Rickie 1992. *Wake Up Little Susie: Single Pregnancy and Race Before Roe v. Wade.* New York: Routledge.

_____ 1994. *The Abortionist: A Woman Against the Law.* New York: The Free Press.

Stacey, Judith 1990. *Brave New Families: Stories of Upheaval in Late Twentieth Century America.* New York:Basic Books.

_____ 1991. "Can There Be a Feminist Ethnography?" in Sherna Berger Gluck and Daphne Patai 1991. *Practice of Oral History.* New York and London: Routledge.

Stanley, Liz and Sue Wise 1991. "Feminist Research, Feminist Consciousness, and Experiences of Sexism," in Mary Margaret Fonow and Judith A. Cook, eds., *Beyond Methodology: Feminist Scholarship as Lived Research.* Blomington and Indianapolis: Indiana University Press.

Stanely, Liz and Sue Wise 1993. *Breaking Out Again.* New York and London: Routledge.

Torres, Aida and Jacqueline Darroch Forrest 1988. "Why Do Women Have Abortions?" *Family Planning Perspectives* 20:169-176.

Townsend, Rita and Ann Perkins 1992. *Bitter Fruit: Women's Experiences of Unplanned Pregnancy, Abortion and Adoption.* Alameda, California: Hunter House.

Turner, Faythe, ed. 1988. *Puerto Rican Writers at Home in the U.S.A: An Anthology*. Seattle: Open Hand Publishing Inc.

Vega, Ana Lydia 1984. "de bipeda desplumada a escritora puertorriquena con E y P machusculas: textimoniou autocensurados," in La torre deo viejo, I, 2, 44–48. Translated and quoted in Diana Velez, ed., 1988, *Reclaiming Medusa: Short Stories by Contemporary Puerto Rican Women*. San Francisco: spinsters/aunt lute.

Velez, Diana ed., 1988. *Reclaiming Medusa: Short Stories by Contemporary Puerto Rican Women*. San Francisco: spinsters/aunt lute.

Walters, Catherine 1984. "Violence Against Women: There Is No Typical Victim," prepared for the Public Education Project of the Illinois Coalition Against Domestic Violence and the Illinois Coalition Against Sexual Assault.

Warner, R. Stephen 1988. *New Wine in Old Wineskins: Evangelicals and Liberals in a Small Town Church*. Berkeley: University of California Press.

Weitzman, Lenore 1985. *The Divorce Revolution*. New York: Free Press.

Wilson, William Julius 1987. *The Truly Disadvantaged: The Inner City, the Underclass, and Public Policy*. Chicago and London: University of Chicago Press.

Zimmerman, Mary K. 1977. *Passage Through Abortion: The Personal and Social Reality of Women's Experiences*. New York: Praeger.

Zinn, Maxine Baca 1989. "Family, Race, and Poverty in the Eighties," *Signs: Journal of Women in Culture and Society* 14: pp. 856–876.

____1990. "Family, Feminism, and Race in America," *Gender and Society* 4: 68–82.

Index of Interviewees

About the Book and Author

Abortion and the right of a woman to control her fertility cross boundaries of race, ethnicity, and social class. In this revealing and in-depth study, Jean P. Peterman focuses on a group of Puerto Rican women in Chicago whose decisions about abortion highlight the contradictions between the sexually conservative ethnic and religious beliefs of this community and the fact that Latina women (including Puerto Rican women) have abortions at a rate one and a half times as high as non-Latinas.

For more than half the women Peterman interviewed, their decision to have an abortion allowed them to maintain opportunities for themselves or to resist male control. Despite their resistance to traditional gender roles, their Puerto Rican identity remains strong.

The term "cultural story," coined by sociologist Laurel Richardson, explains how cultures create and support their social worlds—their cultural and social frameworks as well as beliefs about home, community, sex roles, and family. A "collective story" is an oppositional story—a form of resistance and a catalyst for change.

In this book, the stories recounted by these women involve struggles against barriers instrinsic to their social structure, such as poverty, prejudice, and discrimination, that ultimately shape newfound feelings of independence, inner strength, and control over their own fertility and their lives.

Jean P. Peterman is a visiting assistant professor in the Department of Sociology, Anthropology, and Philosophy at Chicago State University